GROWING UP GREEN
©2017 Khalid Saleem

Published by Hellgate Press

(An imprint of L&R Publishing, LLC)

Hellgate Press
PO Box 3531
Ashland, OR 97520
email: info@hellgatepress.com

Interior & Cover Design: L. Redding
Editng: Cathy Munoz, Jerry Shaw

Cataloging In Publication Data is available from the publisher upon request.
ISBN: 978-1-55571-857-2

Printed and bound in the United States of America
First edition 10 9 8 7 6 5 4 3 2 1

*I dedicate my book to the family and friends
who have always believed in me and to
all the soldiers with whom I proudly served.*

CONTENTS

GROWING UP GREEN

Or How To Survive U.S. Army
Basic Training and Live to Write About It

KHALID SALEEM

HELLGATE PRESS   ASHLAND, OREGON

We are all clay molded by our experiences,
Hardened by the fire of our trials,
And displayed by the way our deeds
Are reflected upon the mirrors of life.

1

Enlisted at Seventeen

ENLISTED AT SEVENTEEN! WOW, EVEN saying it out loud sounds crazy. Whenever I tell people how young I was when I signed up, their initial reaction usually is, "You were a baby!" And to that I say, *I guess I was.*

I was young, but the military was the best decision of my life because I found me. I wasn't ready for college. I wasn't that confident and I was flat-out too lazy to fill out college applications. I spent the better half of my formative years in the "Green." If my first seventeen years with my parents made me a good person, the next ten years I spent in the Green made me a man. In this short book, I share with you tales of my experiences. I hope they tickle your sense of humor and encourage you to have your own adventures and self-discovery.

2

The Decision

SCREECH! "We've stopped." Heavy huffs of breath blow in the vast darkness as heartbeats race faster than a three-year-old on the verge of an ass whooping. Teeth clatter like cymbals in an orchestra, and droplets of sweat draw sounds of thunder to the metal floor. "The fragrance polluting this black hole is called *Ass du Fear* and it is drenched on every last one of us." SKRRREEEK! A rusty metal door slides open and a wave of sunlight floods through, revealing a seventeen-year-old kid holding two duffel bags. Eight silhouettes appear in the light and demand, "Everyone get off my cattle truck!"

****

Wait. Let me back it up a little and explain a few things. My name is Khalid Saleem and up to this point, prior to my enlistment, my name was by far the most exciting thing that had ever happened to me. I come from a family of revolutionists, which is where I got my name. That doesn't explain, however, how in hell we became a military family, but we did!

My path to the Army was as simple as could be. I could go to Ms. Brown's English class, where I didn't do my homework yet again, or take the Armed Services Vocational Aptitude Battery exam, better known in the streets as the ASVAB. To me, it was simple. ASVAB wins!

Due to my lack of interest in filling out college applications, my test scores would be a welcomed sight. When they arrived, I'll never forget the local recruiter calling me into his office and saying, "I've got good news for you my friend. You are smart, lucky, and can choose any job you want."

He had me instantly — hook, line and sinker. Recruiters are kind of like pimps that way, with their perfectly pressed clothes, pearly teeth, slick shiny shoes, and crisp hairdos. They know exactly what their prostitutes need to hear to get them in the streets. Only thing I had to do now was tell my family and girlfriend about this great opportunity. If they could see this as a great opportunity… well, that was another question.

Leading up to that fateful moment, I was sweating bullets and pacing a hole through the pavilion floors of Sunny Isle's outdoor mall. The fear of confronting my parents produced a loop of questions that jogged in my head:

How would they take it?

Will my mom cry?
Would they let me go?

Then I had a brilliant idea. I could run away and fake my own death. It seemed a more appealing option than telling my parents. I ended up not choosing that option and instead took the dollar taxi home. It was a closer call than you'd think. What I can remember from the moment I stepped in the door is that I was shaking in my pants, on the verge of peeing, as I called for the family to come into the living room. We weren't the Cosby family, but everyone came on demand. My father, who had never left the living room to begin with, was already there watching *The Godfather* for the billionth time. You would think it was a sitcom as often as he watched it. My youngest brother, Zayd, waddled over with his chubby self. He was ten years younger than me, so not quite a real person in my eyes yet. Amir, the brother right under me, trudged in, not really wanting to be there, but my mother can be compelling. By compelling I mean my mother dragged him by the earlobe as he winged and, in turn, dragged his size-twelve sneaks along our marble floor.

When everyone was finally in the living room, all wearing "WTF?" expressions, I squirmed and perspired in front of them uncomfortably. I kept saying in my head, *Just blurt it out.* My father, the impatient one in the family, barked out in his gruff DMX voice, "Just say what you want to say!"

Like a kid with Tourette's, I vomited out, "I signed up for the Army!" I covered up my body as if I were protecting myself from a verbal firing squad. Surprisingly, nothing happened. For being the first person in my immediate family to join the military, you'd think there'd be some flopping on the floor like a Southern Baptist church catching the Holy Spirit or at least a question, but nope! Nothing. *No one gave a damn!*

My dad was like, *Cool, one more off the roster, two more to go.* My brothers broke into a flash mob MMA fight as they jostled for my room, and my mom pursed her lips for a quick second and then nodded in acceptance. Yep, no emotional breakdowns or political struggles there, just the boot out the door. I trudged out the room taking quick glances before I exited. In my eyes, I saw someone who was being forgotten before he left. I wondered how my girlfriend would take it next.

The next day I met my girlfriend at school at our third favorite meeting spot, under the steps next to old Rasta Woman's French class. I took the more direct route this time and only waited through five minutes of sweating before saying, with my voice full of a deep bass sound, "Woman, I am going into the Army, and you better like it, woman!" The way it came out of my mouth didn't quite sound like that, but I did tell her, in what ended up being a somewhat bass-like and sheepish voice, that I was joining the Army. Margarita gazed up at me with her beautiful emerald eyes, smiled and said, "Cool, I wouldn't mind talking to them, too."

I was so surprised, not because she was weak or anything like that. She was furthest from an authority-following person than anyone I had ever met, so I was thrilled. I took her to meet my recruiter, but after an hour, she was not impressed. I was sold once again on the promise of the world, which tells you what side of the maturity spectrum I landed on. She asked question after hard-hitting question, such as:

What doors will my military experience open for me when I get out?
Can you assure I can go to college while I am enlisted?
Can you guarantee me my duty station of choice?

I sat in my seat with this stupid, plastered-on grin, frozen with embarrassment as my recruiter just stared daggers back at me. I never broke my character of a smiling, embarrassed politician even as he ushered us out the glass door. If there were any confusion about his displeasure with the conversation, it was cleared up with the hammer of the door lock a second after leaving. Margarita glanced up at me with those emerald eyes of hers and tossed me a quick peck on the cheek. She apologized for interrogating my recruiter and said she'd think about it.

I tried not to look disappointed and smiled, but my veneers could not hide the growing unrest and feeling of melancholy that stole into my heart. Looking back, I realized she was right, and I should have been more concerned about what she asked. The reality then was if you flashed something shiny in my face, I was gonna smile and nod.

The next day Margarita and I met at our second favorite meeting spot next to old man Gonzales' room. His electronics class was always packed because he spoke little

English and gave out lots of "A's." Hence, the alley by his room had little to no traffic. It was the perfect meeting spot. This time she had something to tell me. She sat me down on the step. Nothing good ever happens when someone sits you down. She led with those emerald heart-piercing torpedoes again and chimed out, "I've signed up for the Navy."

Then she went on this long soliloquy that I translated to say, "Their recruiter offered me less shiny things and more assurance of quality of life."

Yeah, like that's important. For the record, though, quality of life is actually a big plus over shiny items. She then serenely asked me with her velvety, perfectly sized hands wrapped around my hand, "Would you come with me to the Navy?"

Whoa!

When I brought up the subject, it wasn't that big of a deal, but when she mentioned it, I couldn't help thinking it was now a huge deal. For one, it wasn't my idea anymore and I had been doing this for me; and, for two, the Navy uniforms sucked and I didn't want to wear them for four years. All that aside, I loved this girl and this was an enormous monkey wrench in the decision-making process. Not only was I wrestling with the decision of should I join the military at all, but also with the decision of whether to join the military for a girl I love.

Days passed and my recruiter was getting restless. He started calling me two times a day. We didn't have cell phones back in those days, but I know it was two times a day by the amount of times my mother screamed at me, "Tell that man stop calling this house, geez!"

I would be lying if I said that the attention wasn't flattering. I mean, someone is treating you like the fate of the Army hinges on your signature. That's exhilarating. Putting my ego to the side, I had to make a decision soon. My recruiter needed me to sign up and join, and Margarita needed to know if she could tell her recruiter to type up those military matrimonies. It was so much pressure that I needed to act fast, which meant I needed to procrastinate just a little more in my world. So I called the funniest person to take my mind off of the situation. My cousin Scot might as well have been my older brother as we were that close. He had caught wind of my dilemma from my mom. Scot wasn't around for most of my senior year angst, but before I could personally catch him up, he blurted out, "Dude! I am so proud of you!"

Scot had wanted to join the military ever since we were kids, but a machete accident to the eye took that dream away when we were eleven. He was now over the moon for me. I had fulfilled one of his dreams and he pretty much saw it as becoming Uncle Sam's nephew because of me. We spoke for hours, mainly about how awesome it was going to be joining the military. He asked me about Margarita. He really liked her and thought that she was good for me. We did take the occasional break so he could talk about his extensive porn collection, but we mostly discussed joining the military. After I hung up with Scot, I knew what I was going to do.

I drove over to Margarita's house on top of a big hill that night. I hated driving up there. My little Dodge Neon would always bottom out going over those craters she called potholes. As I arrived at the top, she was waiting for me outside. She took us to our number one favorite meeting spot, her roof. It was quiet up there. She could get away from the chaos of her teenage life and I could sit next to someone who thought I was important. I took her hand this time and gazed into her eyes. I smiled and then she smiled. I then said, "I can't go with you."

In full teenage dramatization layered with a little Korean pop music score, she kissed me and whispered, "I know." We lay there gazing at the stars a little longer, not saying anything but saying everything. We knew nothing would ever be the same.

****

The next day, I honored my deal and told my recruiter I was ready to be on the team. He beamed with a smile that lit up the one-man recruiting station. He then grabbed my hand with a handshake similar to a vise grip. I smiled to hide my wincing. My recruiter was so overjoyed that he dropped everything he was doing and said, "Let's celebrate! How does Chinese sound to you?"

Back then, in the Virgin Islands, Chinese food was like eating at the Waldorf Astoria since it was so expensive. I snickered and replied, "Yeah, De'man!"

It might seem like a lot of factors played into my decision, but at the end of the day, it was really simple. The Army wanted me. I felt a new type of pride this time, the pride of making a grown-man decision. For most of us, who we are now is really a domino effect of a series of decisions that start in our teens. This was the first string in my series.

.

3

Picking My Job

YOU PROBABLY WANT ME TO GET BACK to the story about me on the verge of being slaughtered by a pack of drill sergeants, and I will. First, I have to tell you about the best part of signing up for the military. It's picking your job! Well, that's if you got higher than a fifty on the ASVAB, which was the magic score to get back in 1998.

See the ASVAB is the SAT of the military and organizes the military folk into three job classes:

> 1) the "I'm Hella Book Smart and Can Change The World" jobs (the sh!# you get in Wikileaks);
>
> 2) the "I'm Smart Enough To Make Sure The Military Maintains" jobs (the stuff you see on commercials); and
>
> 3) the "I May Not Have Had the Highest Score, But Dammit I Keep The World Safe" jobs (the stuff you see in movies).

Yours truly pulled off such a feat with a score of 51, better than average, and was thrust into the middle class of the job pool. I was particularly geeked by such a score because my recruiter told me that I had the pick of the litter, which meant I had the safe jobs. This pleased my mom very much. Even though I entered the military during a time when there was no major war, things could pop off at any time. My mom knew the reality of the world better than I did, so if I could pick a cake job, that would make her feel more secure.

Being a Virgin Island resident, I had to travel to Puerto Rico for my Military Entrance Processing Station (MEPS). This is where you find out if the military wants your ass or not. The perks of your MEPS visit include:

> *Eye exam game show*—It's not really a game show, but if you fail, you are rewarded with ugly brown glasses that only Mr. Magoo could love.
>
> *Getting your testicles cupped*—Not as fun as it sounds.
>
> *Inspection for flat footedness disease*—Your recruiter tells you exactly how to cheat on this test.

After cruising through the first two medical exams, it was time for the only examination that I was worried about, checking of my flat-ass feet. I heard horror stories about people not getting in on the make-up of their feet. They were not able to complete road marches in war, so it was a big deal. My recruiter told me all the tricks to beat the system, but my feet might have been designed by a Lego maker. There is absolutely no arch. I walked into the examination room, half on my tiptoes and the other half on my heel. I waddled in like a giant black man impersonating a king penguin. The nurse gasped to hold back his chuckle. I placed the pressure on the outside of my feet to fool the examiner, as I'd been coached. I stood there against the wall proud and tall with my gut tucked in for some odd reason, like that was gonna help. The nurse circled around my feet similar to a seagull looking at trash. As he looked closer, I cupped my feet more. And more. And more. I cupped my feet so high to the point when he couldn't hold back his laughter anymore. He cried out, chuckling, "Dude! Please just lay your feet normal. I see about a hundred of these a day and this has to be the most obvious."

His honest reaction forced me to laugh a little and relax. I flattened down my feet and then he blurted out, "Damn!"

I immediately stiffened back up upon his reaction. The nurse then said, "On second thought, try to fool me just a little bit."

So I found a happy balance of broad-jump stance and plié dance position. You know what? It worked. The nurse gave me the stamp of approval and it was showtime, the part every young recruit can't wait for: da job!

This was it, the moment of truth. My heart thumped through my jersey as I stared forward, cracking my neck. My fate lay behind a metal door. As I walked through that gateway, thoughts rushed through my brain.

What jobs did I qualify for?
Where would I go for Basic?
What were the exact lyrics to Smash Mouth's song "Allstar?"

The last question was about the hot band of that summer and oddly comforting to me somehow.

I slid into a tiny gray cubicle and eased down into a chair that felt like it was padded by plywood on top of more plywood. The only advantage that gave me, as tight as my ass had become from nerves, was the plywood-cushioned seats raised me three feet higher and I could look at the gigantic Army staff sergeant across from me at eye level. He had to be seven feet tall and forged from an Abercrombie clay-model mold. I was trembling as he seemed to flash me a Stepford smile with his pearly white teeth. It was the kind of awkward smile that you might get from a robot trying to analyze you. So I did the only thing you could do back. I eked out my own smile, only I resembled a constipated dog asking to be mercifully put to sleep. After a twenty-second smile-off, he finally broke the silence with, "Congratulations, Mr. Saleem, on choosing the greatest Army in the world! Now let's complete this journey and make sure you get the job of your dreams."

He spoke in a fast-food takeout voice and I fully

expected him to ask me if I wanted fries to go with that dream job. He reached under his desk, pulled out a gray binder, rested it on the desk, and said, "This is the binder of dreams, Mr. Saleem."

He then tossed me a creepy, used-car salesman wink and smile, opening "the binder of dreams." My heart fluttered as the binder glowed when it opened. Sergeant Abercrombie said in his Stepford fast-food takeout voice, "Aha! I have just the job for you."

My eyes widened and my ass raised me up even higher on my seat, surpassing imagination. Before he could utter another word, I suddenly had a calming and clear thought navigate through the sea of jumbled thoughts. They were the wise words of my recruiter. He warned me in his best G.I. Joe voice, "Don't forget to ask questions. Take your time. Understand the clear description of your job."

Sadly, however, that wasn't my soldier way. The Abercrombie sergeant flashed a smile and said, "How would you like this job?" He showed me the description in the book. That's when hard, fast, gut instinct was the technique I chose to use. So after only twenty minutes of listening to the most glamorous description of the most mundane job known to man, my interview concluded.

Wearing a big grin on my face, I shook the flashy sergeant's manicured hand and walked towards the door. Once I was out of eyesight, I broke out the George Jefferson strut and twirled out of the door, back into the waiting room. I strutted a little more for the audience of the waiting room. They gawked and gazed with their judgmental mouths pursed up and noses in the air, but I didn't care and moved on. You would have thought I'd just won "The Price Is Right" or had selected the most amazing job in the known universe with the swagger I was exuding. In all actuality, it couldn't have been further from the truth. I had chosen the Ford Pinto of jobs, communications specialist. This was on the lower end of the middle-class job spectrum.

My recruiter eventually sprinted over to me with his hands in the air, asking for news. As I showed him my slick dance steps, his smile and slight fist pump said it all, "another soldier in the stable." That smile quickly dissipated when I cockily told him my M.O.S (military occupational specialty): "Guess who has two thumbs and just became the Army's new communications specialist?"

He retorted with an, "Excuse me?" Then he proceeded to turn beet red to the point that I thought he was going to explode. I don't remember the exact words he said to me that day, but it went kinda like, "That was a crap job! (Some Spanish bad words). Wire dog! Don't you listen? Let me talk to this mother-(four-letter variation)! (Some more Spanish bad words of the really, really bad variety)."

And then he was finished. Every muscle in my body had contracted and I stood there staring at him the same way you do when your mom or pop shot you a quick slap because you said something rude. He could barely look at me but somehow found the strength and shot me a soul-strangling gaze. My recruiter then shouted, "Don't move!"

So I didn't and he stormed back into the room that I had just left victoriously. I stood there for what seemed like hours (five minutes tops) with my pride down for the ten count and drowning in my own puddle of embarrassment. *Tick, tock, tick, tock* rung in my head as I paced back and forth from chair to chair in the waiting room. Then after my billionth or so pace, I turned around and, like magic, my recruiter had returned. This time he was grinning, his eyebrows had leveled and his face was the creamy-cool vanilla color that whispered peace. His calm appearance told me that everything was going to be all right. He straightened my body up and told me some brief instructions, "Go in and sit down. He'll do the rest."

So I strolled in and sat inside that same cubicle, but this time Sergeant Abercrombie's face cringed with fear. That is the moment I found out that my recruiter was actually the freaking man! I was his proud soldier as the shaken Sergeant Abercrombie reached under his desk this time and pulled out a brand new book. This binder was blue and I may have heard Gabriel's horn when he opened it up. This was a whole new catalog of jobs for me. I was still in the middle- class realm, but damn it, I was on the *bougie* side now.

Sergeant Abercrombie laid out the top ten jobs and the packages that he could offer me. He pointed out the most favorable one first, which was medical supply specialist in Ft. Rucker, Alabama. He glared intensely at me and, like before, I was a little confused and glared back at him with one eyebrow raised. His face cringed in frustration and he nodded, saying, "Great choice, Mr. Saleem."

I squinted in confusion and replied, "Thank you?" in a questioning voice.

He rushed and pulled out paperwork from his manila folder and then proceeded to grab my hand and sign for me. I don't remember fighting that much because by this point I didn't know what was the right thing to do, and he was making it easier for me. After the deed had been done, he smiled and smugly said, "Thank you, Mr. Saleem, and I hope you enjoy your time at Ft. Rucker, Alabama, as the newest member of its medical supply team." He nodded. Then I nodded. Then he ushered me out the door.

The first person I saw on my way out was my recruiter with folded arms and a sly snicker on his face. He was a man that I had been convinced did not have my best interest in mind.

Reflecting back now, I don't know what my life would be without a man who was more than my recruiter. He was definitely my guardian angel.

4

Saying Goodbye

MY LAST SUMMER BEFORE BASIC TRAINING WAS ONE of nothingness. I mean it. I did absolutely nothing. When you are going to college, you prep: get clothes, books, and put your finances in order. However, when you go to the military, you screw around to a legendary degree.

My Pre-Basic Training Schedule:

1. Party
2. Sleep till 3:00 p.m.
3. Watch TV
4. Play Video Games
5. Party
6. Sleep till 3:00 p.m

Now just loop that a gazillion more times, and you get the point.

The one thing you do have to do of any importance before you leave is saying your goodbyes. So with a couple of days left of freedom, I set upon my last march of goodbyes. Let me tell you, they were pretty awesome! People treat you like they will never see you again. I mean parties, gifts, and honesty. The last perk might not work for everybody, but honesty works for me. You find out what people really think and feel about you.

Everything was going great in my final lap tour before basic training, but I pushed my going away visit to one place too many. The day before I left for basic, I headed to my old high school with my younger brother, Amir, I guess for one last stroke of the old ego. I made an illegal right turn into my old school, one I had made a million times before with no problem, and then…

BOOM! CRASH! In an instant, I was lying flat, outside of my vehicle. I got on my knees by the driver side of my shiny red '97 Dodge Neon, clutching my chest and hoping for death. My car's rear end was love-tapped by the Hulk and my life expectancy lowered by half. My father was going to kill me the day before I left for Army boot camp. No, this wasn't his car but rather my grandmother's. She had recently passed away, so this was an inheritance gift and we weren't inheritance-type people. This was special and I screwed it up. To this day, I swear a Mack truck hit me, but as I cradled the asphalt with my knees and my head in a hazy fog, I am almost certain I saw a friend of mine peek in to check on me and say, "Sorry," before peeling off in the car.

I reached out and said, "Please kill me."

A death by his hands would have saved me the anguish of telling my father.

To best describe my father in a nutshell, think of the biggest and scariest creature you can imagine, and then give it the intellect of Einstein, the charm of Dracula, and the temper of Mr. Hyde. Then after you have conjured up this super monster, throw out everything you know about that creature and imagine the kindest person you know. My father was a walking contradiction who could be both terrifying and gentle, but also consistently irrational. My father's wild card personality is what made this car crash a real dilemma.

My brother and I sat on our respective sides of our car in the middle of the empty school parking lot, not saying a peep. He peeked over several times to catch a glimpse of my lifeless body as I stared aimlessly into space. My brother and I weren't close in the conventional way, but more in the prison cellmates type of way. All in all, he was concerned for my well-being, but he was also relieved that it wasn't him in hot water. He broke the silence by saying, "It could be worse. Dad could be here right now. Please don't tell him I was with you. I've been on a good streak lately and don't need the heat."

I just shot him the glare of death as the Lord held me back from smacking the teeth out his mouth. He felt the anger radiating from my body and replied, "But I'm sure you'll be good. Don't worry too much."

My brother was right and no help to me as a witness. He had not seen anything from the crash as his head hit the dashboard and made him fall back to the driver's seat cushion. I was gonna have to walk this path alone again. We stayed at the parking lot long enough to watch the sunset. I don't know if my imminent death made me even more sensitive, as I just marveled at the orange rays fraternizing with the blue skies illuminating their pillowy white breasts. If this were to be my death, this was the last image I wanted to see. Finally, I knew I was ready. It was time to man up. So I decided to do the brave act and tell my mom.

What you should know about my mother is just this: she was our savior. The amount of ass whipping that she rescued us from was countless. She might as well have been Harriet Tubman for the many times she hid us from a spanking. She was a kind, artsy and intellectual revolutionist, who made growing up easy and without pressures of lofty expectations. She was more concerned with us being good people than having an extraordinary occupation. My mother was the first line of defense from the certain execution that my father was ready to dole out on a daily basis. Yep, in Mom's hands, all this misunderstanding would be handled. I felt sure of it. After all, I was the victim, the survivor of a heinous crime, and she would make that clear to my dad.

I pulled into the driveway. My dad was already home, so I could strategically park the car at a flattering angle. As I pulled in, however, the security lights' bright rays rushed passed my car's windshield, finding me like a criminal in hiding. My brother dashed out from the car with little more than a *Good luck, dude.* As I shielded the blast of light from my eyes, a figure appeared. I thought it was my dad at first and a stampede of fear trampled over my soul. The figure moved closer, eclipsing the light. It was my mother. I exhaled all the oxygen in my lungs. She waved at me with a warm smile. *A friendly gesture, yes.* I waved her over to sit in the car.

She came and did not ask me any questions. That's when I knew my ally would make everything right. It didn't quite go how I thought it would.

"*You did what?* You have to tell your father." She paused and said, "Wow, he's gonna kill you."

The gravity of my mistake suddenly hit me in that situation; my savior might not be able to save me. I had to ask, "Mommy, please!"

Okay, I admit it, beg.

"Please, Mommy! Talk to him for me."

She stared at me, grimacing, clearly wrestling with what to do. I wanted to be brave, promise, but this was hard and I didn't want my last goodbye with my dad to involve him screaming at me. My mother nodded begrudgingly and gave me a hug, as moms do, and was just happy her favorite son was alive (*it's good to be the writer in the family*). She said she would tell him after our last family dinner. After the hard stuff had been settled, I walked my mother to the back of the car and her face peeled up as if she had just seen a dead body with its torso mutilated. She blurted out, "Oh my God! On second thought, maybe you should fake your own death." The boost of confidence was going to make for a great last dinner.

All of us sat at the table, family-style. My mother fixed baked turkey thighs, baked rice and peas, and Brussels sprouts, all my favorites. This was definitely a meal prepared for a dead man walking, or in this case, sitting. We weren't a sit-down-and-eat-at-the-table kinda family, so there was more mowing down of food than conversation. My mother who was the classiest one of the bunch, serving a lifelong sentence of taking care of Neanderthals, stood up to give a speech. She said, "Khalid, you have been the most amazing kid to raise. One who has always made the right decisions and always been responsible."

My mom began to cry. I thought, *This is perfect!* The whole table civilized up and was at her attention. She continued on, "I am so proud of you and pray you make it through this rigorous journey."

The speech took a drastic turn and right into a roast. Alarms went off in my head. *What, you don't think I'm gonna make it?* Everyone nodded right along like, "true dat." My savior kept going on, spewing honesty as if she were drunk, but we were Muslim and that, unfortunately, wasn't the case.

"You're not the toughest kid I have, and, quite frankly, a little sensitive, but I am confident that you will give basic training a good run for its money. Cheers to you, my beautiful son."

In unison, they raised their cups and glasses, "Cheers!" I reluctantly raised mine barely above my mouth, uttered a half-hearted *Cheers* and chugged my cider. We continued eating, but worse than the accident and probably more painful than my dad being angry at me, had to be the lack of belief everyone had in me. *Was I that pathetic?*

Right after dinner, my mother spoke to my father in their bedroom. A soldier-to-be, I did the manly thing and hid in the other room as she broke the news to him. I did not fear the outcome as much anymore. I had more pressing issues on my mind. *The total and utter disappointment of a man I was to them. They had no faith in me.* Then I heard a couple of F-bombs flying during that conversation and the fear crept back. Yep, that was my first real taste of a combat zone. It seemed they had finished when it got all quiet. I tried to enter the room, thinking the worst was over and I should apologize. My mother quickly ushered me back out, saying, "Too soon."

An hour later he came out and I expected fireworks, but what followed was worse than any yelling. My father completely shunned me. I was officially dead to the man. He wouldn't even look at me, and that is when I knew this would be the hardest goodbye.

The next day at the airport, everybody was there to send me off, except my father. I waited and waited, scanning the landscape, hoping for a peek of the giant. Meanwhile, emotions flew around the airport like the end to a Tyler Perry movie. It was time to set off on my journey and still no dad. Everyone gave final hugs and kisses. My aunt and grandmother wept quietly.

My brother, Amir, gave me a real hug, not his usual one-arm-and-handshake man hug, but a real mushy two-arm squeeze and embrace. My mother drenched my cheek with tears, snot and kisses. As I was about to shove off, I saw my pop's blue Bronco pull up to the side of the airport. He dashed over to me. Well, I guess as fast a dash as any 300-plus-pound man can dart over to a person. He pulled me aside and said, "Sorry I'm late. I had a meeting, then ran over. I would never miss you leaving no matter how mad I am at you." Then he told me something I had heard only one other time from my nana, "Parents chew you up, son, but they will never spit you out.

You hear me?"

I nodded because when my father spoke I always listened. He went on to tell me that I would pay for the car from my first check and said, "Honestly, what is money when you have your life?" My dad then started doing something that I had only heard of in myths. These droplets started escaping from his eye wells. It took me a second as I stood there bewildered, head cocked to the side, and blinking. I finally processed that he was shedding a couple of tears, a sight as rare as seeing a unicorn wearing chaps. This was an earth-shattering event that I can now talk about since he has passed away. Sure, I was still a little bitter about the fact that these people thought I was leaving for my death because they thought I wasn't tough enough. The thing is, goodbyes aren't about the sad things but about the celebration of the past. My family expressed some hard honesty, and I love honesty no matter how much it hurts. It was my job to prove them wrong now. As I walked through the terminal doors on July 31, 1998, my Army career was born. I set off knowing that the best goodbyes are always saved for last

5

Amnesty

SOME 2,153 MILES BY PLANE and bus is what it took to get to the destination of Ft. Leonard Wood, Missouri, and I still hadn't quite reached the Basic Training site. In the dead of the night, we arrived. The landscape was pitch black with the only source of light coming from beady flashlight bulbs that barely illuminated these old cabin-like buildings with chipped-white siding and dookie-brown shingles.

The scene looked reminiscent of something out of *Full Metal Jacket* meets *Friday the 13th*. Wiping the half-asleep debris out of our eyes, we got ushered out of the bus with the care of newborn kittens. These people had the hospitality of monastery priests as they kindly led us into a large bay room with standard issue, black folding-picnic chairs. I thought this was more like basic training-lite than what I saw in the movies. The kind people who led us off the bus asked if we needed refreshments and offered to carry our green duffel bags. We all accepted without hesitation. There were about seventy recruits in the hall and we sipped on our water as if we were at a resort. The jokes were flying and giggles were running through our eardrums. I pulled out a pocket-size prom picture of Margarita and whispered, "I guess I will make it out of this alive after all."

I kissed it and slid it back into my pocket. Then things changed gradually, and I noticed those helpful soldiers who had taken good care of us slowly creep out of the room, using the fog of euphoria as their cover. No more than five minutes later, I was saying, "Those Summabitches!" as those no-good, two-faced and extremely nice-to-your-face bastards switched out with some legitimate assholes. At 2 a.m., there were a trio of jerks dressed in crisply pressed, green Army fatigues. They might as well have been triplets of evil the way they were dressed the same, and now they were up in our faces, barking commands and threats. My favorite was, "Don't eyeball me, soldier!" Followed immediately by, "You better look at me, Private!"

I quickly realized that you couldn't win with these guys. We went from total glee to young men and women on the verge of tears. The line that broke us down to our knees was the talk of an amnesty box. This was a handcrafted, wooden box that looked like it was constructed in a wood-shop class, nailed onto the wall with two-bit handiwork and embroidered with block lettering that read, "All contraband in here."

Basically, if you possessed anything that wasn't Army-related, then drop it in there. For the record, not Army-related meant everything that could make you smile. So one by one, trembling young men and women dropped items that meant something to them into a box as they walked through a wooden door. I mean, I saw everything ranging from cigarettes and family pictures to porn magazines, condoms and various items that I'll just categorize as crazy sh!#.

When it got to my turn, one of the evil triplets looked me in the eye and asked me straight up if I had anything I wanted to turn in. I stared right back to the side of his face, barely making eye contact, and paused. I fidgeted in my pocket, massaging the picture with my fingertips, but also feeling itchy to confess and turn it in. He stared at me a little longer as if he wanted to stare my conscience into submission. I slowly pulled my hand out and said, "No, sir."

He quickly retorted in a loud bark, "Sir? I work for a living, son! No, Sergeant!" Fumbling and stammering, I replied, "Yes, sir-geant! I mean, no, sir! I mean, no, Sergeant!"

With a sinister smile, he said, "That's good, because if you did have contraband and didn't tell me, then that'd be grounds for sending you home. And a pretty thing like you doesn't want go home yet, do you?"

Wide-eyed and with a slight shiver now, I flashed a nervous smile and shook my head. He immediately shouted at me, "Don't eyeball me, soldier!"

He then flashed me a smile that lingered in a crazy way, and not the friendly type. He allowed me to proceed on by. I kept on thinking, *I am free right now, but for how long?*

That night I lay on my bunk in an open bay full of newbies. We were packed in there like prisoners from Ellis Island. It was too late to talk, but not too late to listen to the midnight snores of fatigued travelers or the whimpering of exhausted false bravery. I pulled the photo from my pocket, sitting on top of my bunk. I stared at Margarita for a second, or maybe an hour to be truthful. She left for her Basic Training a couple of weeks before me. I was longing to talk to her and tell her how much had changed in the millisecond we had been apart. She always believed in me. I knew if I was gonna survive this experience that I needed her belief in me, but I also knew getting in trouble would shorten my basic training mortality. The words of that evil-triplet sergeant had gotten to me. *Would they find my photo or was it all a bluff?* This was only the first night and I was already going through the wars mentally. I wasn't the only one though, and if there were a camera in that bay room filming us all simultaneously, then it would capture us all going through our own dramas.

In the thick of night, armed only with my flashlight, I tiptoed out of our cabin building, across the field, through the reception area and to the foyer where I found myself in front of the old, wooden amnesty box. I opened my hand to reveal my beautiful Margarita's face now crumpled and creased by the pressure of my nervous palm. I took one last gaze at two young naive kids on their prom night and closed my eyes, taking in the memories of that night. I opened my eyes and surveyed the landscape of my new existence. I gave one last kiss to my Margarita and slotted it into the abyss. I figured with everyone letting go of the physical things of their past, ready for a rebirth, I might as well do the same. I would have to feed off her strength through my memory of something that probably, in reality, wasn't that perfect but now seemed immaculate to me. I just prayed that her support, embedded in my soul, could prop me up for at least now. I traveled back through the reception area, back through the field, in the front door of the cabin and back up my rickety bunk that squeaked every time I moved. I reached inside my bag and pulled out my small, Army camouflaged-green notebook purchased specifically for basic training to begin writing under the light of my flashlight. I wasn't worried about anyone waking, as we were all still awake or too exhausted to care about noise-light discipline. I was so compelled by the emotions brought on by change that I had to write a poem expressing my situation, and it went a little like this.

"Captivity"

Captivity
Locked in chains with mental restraints on my brain
Having debates of should I stay, should I go AWOL,
or should I just wait. My head's very hectic
Scared of people being kleptic
Sure I know that they're cool
But some people's sketchy side are shining through
Fixation on formation
They love keeping stuff basic
No individuality
They'd prefer multiplicity
For fear of rebels among the community
But sadly my life and my experiences
Prove I'm in captivity

6

In-Processing

BEFORE YOU ENTER THE REALM OF FIRE and brimstone known as Basic Training, you must first get your gear. The military wants you to look good while you are being tormented. What the commercials didn't prep me for was the ass shot. Yes you heard me right, the shot in the old rear end with penicillin.

In processing, there was a two-day event with the main event being the ass shot. So before that, you have forty-seven hours to get all the gear you needed at random, brown-stained military warehouses before the old poker. Loads of fun, trust me. This is the time where you get to bond and gel with your new co-workers before the bullets start firing. You get the normal version of them and not the stressed out, hormone-driven version you get to know and love even more. The background of the recruits was so dramatically different:

ex-football stars, people looking for college money, parents looking for a break, white supremacists, college geniuses trying to find themselves, strippers and even the occasional patriot.

Yeah, I always wonder why there aren't more movies about Basic Training. A collective group of motley characters like that would be Oscar-worthy, I reckon. The first person I met in Basic Training was Malachi Scott, a soldier with two first names, and loads of opinions. Back then, I was particularly shy and Malachi spotted me from across the cafeteria as he was holding court at his table, entertaining a bunch of other recruits. He bopped over as I sat in the corner and looked like a sick refugee in a holding cell. The first thing he did when he got over to me was, slap! He was one of those aforementioned ex-football players. His slap on my arm shrugged all 180 pounds of me and nearly knocked me off my chair. Malachi wasn't a big dude by any means. I was taller than him, but he was stocky and had masculine strength that I did not. Once I got my balance back, I sheepishly waved at him and said, "Hi, man, my name is Khalid."

He laughed and teased me, using a thick Jamaican accent, "Hey, mon, you wan come over deh and sit wit a couple of us?"

A little bewildered why he was talking like that, I said, "Sure."

At the table, I met the two Thompsons, Katrice and Henry, not related but both funny as hell. I also met Brownlow and Achee, those rare breed patriots that could care less about college money and had dreamed about the military since they were in their G.I. Joe undies. The last person to round out the table was Tia, a goddess who, even without makeup, was clearly a model who had taken a wrong turn into the military. I sat there and listened to their fast-moving conversation about things I had no knowledge of. They were way more worldly than I was and it had nothing to do with my geographical upbringing, rather everything to do with my sheltered upbringing. I simply sat there taking it in as I tried to catch up on five years of back education.

They went on about sex, race and pop culture as my head swiveled from person to person, trying to process. If I could just fake the funk just a little bit longer, I would be okay. Then the conversation switched to the ass shot and I perked up, thinking this is some pertinent stuff.

Malachi said, "I heard the ass shot felt like you were being poked by jagged rusty nails in the ass."

My face froze and vibrated with pressure, thinking *holy sh!#!* Katrice jumped in, "That is a load of horse sh!#!"

I sighed and smirked as I stabilized.

Katrice quickly followed with, "I heard it was even worse than that. I heard it was like having an ice pick shoved into your butt cheek.

I turned pale and surveyed the table for any objections, but nada. Everyone nodded like what she was saying was gospel. The cadre came back in and called us to formation. Everyone dashed off except for me. I couldn't help but think, *What was the point of this torture?* I could only hope now that this day could draw out until a nuclear war broke out just on our base, henceforth canceling the shot. What can I say? I'm an optimist.

The only bright side so far to the day was that we were issued our smart cards. This turned out to be my favorite part of in-processing. The smart card is a system eerily based on the one that prisons use. You know the one where they issue you a debit card with a preset amount of dollars on it. You then use it to buy all the goods you will need to survive for the next nine weeks. Your first trip to the commissary turns into an episode of "Supermarket Sweep." Everyone spends what little cash they get like it is the apocalypse.

I was no different as the only thing that could keep my mind off of what was happening was to shop. Sure, you weren't shopping for glamorous merchandise like Echo Jeans or Coogi sweaters, but trust me, survival makes you look at a flashlight way differently. Aisle after aisle, I dumped anything that looked like it could make me look the part of a soldier in my cart. I tossed in a camouflaged covered notebook. *How crazy is that? Does that make the words tougher?* The toughest aisle had to be the underwear aisle because it made me think of the ass shot. I cringed at the sight of the ugly brown undies ironically situated next to camouflage Band-Aids. I calmly slid a box of those Band-Aids in the basket, thank you very much. I must have burnt through the two-hundred dollars they put on my card within ten minutes.

As the day went on, I got fitted for uniforms, listened to briefings, ate my last normal meal before Basic really started, and listened to more briefings. The hours flew by like an excruciatingly long dream, but all dreams must end and the time for the booty shot had come.

The waiting game was over and we were packed into

the little waiting room that had the eerie feel of an ER holding bay. The room was lined wall to wall with soldiers shivering and sweating. The worst of us waited in a line outside the plain pine door. The door opened periodically and as eight slid in the door, eight hobbled out. Worried looks danced along our faces every time that pine door regurgitated another fallen brethren. Until, finally, my time had arrived, my fifteen seconds of fame to stand outside the door of death. As it had done before, the door hinges flew open and eight lifeless bodies were ejected with eight more going inside, compelled to follow the voice of authority. One by one we filed in, until the eighth man was called, and *it wasn't me!*

The rule was eight in and no more, and I hadn't made it until the next rotation, which right now felt like an eternity. *What?* The door hadn't closed as normal. It just remained half- open like a wormhole in space. A voice called out of the vortex and said, "Come on in. You made it this far and we still have room."

I screamed, "What the F…" Actually, that response was just in my mind. I nodded, saying, "Yes, Sergeant," but I very much meant the first phrase in my subtext.

When I entered, I noticed that the room was not huge at all. It was just big and comfortable enough for eight males and a doctor. With me entering and taking the ninth spot, the room got a little more intimate. There wasn't a whole lot of instructions, just, "You're going to be sore for a little bit. Turn around, drop your pants to your ankles and bend over."

Writing this down now, it plays like a scene from *The Shawshank Redemption* without the good scenes. From my

million-dollar view as the ninth man, I looked down and
saw every head flinch as the jab of the needle drew blood
with every poke. A painful exclamation of "OUGH!" left
their pursed mouths, one after the other, getting closer
until they were just one "ough" away from me. I relaxed
my ass and bit my bottom lip, and ough it came. I'd like to
tell you that it was overrated and I galloped out the room
like a stag, but in truth, I wobbled like an SUV driving on
a doughnut spare tire. I gazed across the room to see
nothing but a massacre of soldiers.

As the penicillin shot was the last thing for the day, I
came back to base with the second rotation. It was a long,
painful ride in the van that day with the load of us leaning
to one ass cheek. Feeling at my lowest since I had arrived,
I walked with the cadre into the barracks. The barracks
were alive and one recruit, this short Puerto Rican dude
with midnight-black sheen hair, was even getting a haircut
from another recruit. The only problem with that was we
weren't allowed to. The cadre shut down the short-lived
barber shop. This left the one recruit in the chair with half
his head bald and the other furnished with his bouncy jet-
black Puerto Rican follicles. He was devastated and the lot
of us also got in trouble. We were sent to bed early. I sat
on top of my bunk that night thinking that my ass might
hurt, but the lesson was things could always be worse. Just
look at Rico Baldy.

7

Drill Sergeants and Punishments

I HAD A STRICT DAD GROWING UP, WHO was definitely a
character, but my drill sergeants took it to another
level. They were the Legion of Doom, comprised of ten
drill sergeants and a maniacal evil mastermind, the First
Sergeant (1SG).

First Sergeant Snur: He was five-foot nothing, big-eared
and horseshoe bald with a tattooed scowl on his face.
Snur had an evil demeanor and his actions revealed that
he would rather see the world crash and burn than ever
show kindness to a recruit. No one knows much about
his origins besides that he was born a jerk, but he did
have a Ranger tab on his uniform, which said he was a

badass.

Head Drill Sergeant Buchanan: He was the nerdy black guy who took the super-human serum and came up. He had a bit of a lisp. It was easy to underestimate him, but that was a mistake because he had a chip on his shoulder, probably from being made fun of as a teenager, and would go from zero to sixty real quick.

The First Platoon

Drill Sergeant Burress: Burress exhibited racist tendencies as he told little Williams, an African-American female from Alabama with the niceties of a Southern belle, that she better fix her nappy hair or the whole platoon would get smoked (forced to do physical punishment). His pastime was nitpicking at the African-American females in his platoon. On the flip side, and if you could look beyond his racist shortcomings, Burress could train the hell out of his soldiers, and was a dynamo soldier himself. His platoon was consistently squared away, ready to go, and was always ahead of what was going on.

Drill Sergeant Superman: His real name was Drill Sergeant Kent, but we nicknamed him Superman. He was white, with rippling muscles, a chiseled chin, and a million-dollar haircut. He was pretty blasé about most things. The most interesting thing about him was that he was always disappearing with our commander (a woman) for long stretches of time during training. I guess it makes sense why we didn't see much of him, or her, even after the eighth week.

The Second Platoon

Drill Sergeant Spivey: As drill sergeants go, none could possibly be more corrupt than Drill Sergeant Spivey. He was tall, gangly, and had a buzz cut that came packaged with a constant devilish smirk. He was the bad boy of the drill sergeant crew, as he was always late and always had an "I don't give a damn" look on his face. His mantra was, "If you ain't cheating, you ain't trying." It was like Donald Trump was training you. Looks, however, can be deceiving. You had to pay attention on certain days when he would wear his uniform with his patches sewed on. He was the most decorated soldier of the drill sergeant bunch, sporting a Ranger Tab, an Expert Field Infantry badge, an Air Assault badge and an Airborne badge. Hell, there might have been a Boy Scout patch there, too, he was so decked out with badges.

Drill Sergeant Coleman: She was an African American who didn't take crap from anyone. She was so short that she could be considered a dwarf. Implications about race, gender and stature were not lost on her, however. She was constantly trying to prove herself. She commanded respect from her peers and could strike fear in the hearts of all the new recruits.

Drill Sergeant Graham: Ever meet the living embodiment of unpredictability? Well, his name was Drill Sergeant Graham, a slightly overweight and bespectacled psychopath. You never knew what role he was playing when you encountered him. One second, you might have your friendly neighborhood-watch guy and the next, Charles Manson. The horn-rimmed glasses and the sinister canyon-wide smile didn't help either. He was the scariest drill sergeant out of all because there was a 50/50 chance that he might just slip and kill ya.

The Third Platoon

Drill Sergeant Boon: He was, by far, the smoothest and coolest, high-profile drill sergeant of the bunch. He was a confident black man from the streets of Philadelphia. His shiny bald head, clean ten-gallon hat, freshly pressed battle dress uniform (BDU) and Kiwi black- polished, shiny boots made him the poster child for what the Army could do for you. He also had the most positive attitude of all the drill sergeants. Boon had a knack for convincing his soldiers that getting smoked by him was only making them stronger. They often repeated his mantra, "Getting smoked is only improving me mentally and physically, as pain is just weakness leaving the body."

Third Platoon was kind of like a willing, brainwashed cult with Drill Sergeant Boon as its leader.

Drill Sergeant Chow: He was also part of the dynamic duo. If Drill Sergeant Boon was Batman, then Drill Sergeant Chow was a tiny Batman with a bigger attitude. He was a five-foot, four-inch walking smoke machine that gave hell to everybody. Drill Sergeant Chow was a second generation Asian American from California and loved everything there was to love about the military.

What he loved most, though, was smoking the life out of you for the smallest infractions. He truly believed in weeding out the weak, and when you saw his Ford F-150 pull up to the front of the barracks, you exorcised the weak out of you fast.

The Fourth Platoon

Drill Sergeant Mitchell: I have heard this saying before and, trust me, I think it is true: *the quiet ones are always the scary ones.* Well, Drill Sergeant Mitchell could fit that. At first, she appeared like a mother hen, a nurturing mother who would listen to you and make sure you were doing what you were supposed to, but then when you stepped the slightest bit out of line, she would go ape sh!#. Yep, that was her. She was my drill sergeant and though we did not see her much in our rotation, when she was there, she made her presence felt. She was the Queen Bee and you were in her hive.

Drill Sergeant Bauer: If you were to splice the DNA of Katniss Evergreen, Chuck Norris and Jason Bourne, and then cultivate a human being from that, not only would you have the toughest human person in the world, but you would also have Drill Sergeant Bauer. He was also my drill sergeant, and though I am biased in his favor, I also heard other drill sergeants rave about his awesomeness. He was a demanding drill sergeant who asked you to bleed for him because he would bleed for you. He would only smoke you if you had it coming, but also to make sure you knew how to avoid it from coming in the first place.

The Punishment Chart

I had seen my fair share of punishments, but I hadn't seen anything before I got to Basic Training. Here is the punishment chart in full glory for you:

Talk to the fish take in the chow hall—*forever*
Stay in the front lean and rest position —*forever*
Stand in parade rest —*forever*
Stand at attention —*forever*
Talk to the imaginary monkey in the tree —*forever*
Run laps around the building —*forever*

The great thing about the military is that if you refuse or don't complete the punishment to standard, you get a punishment for the punishment.

What's the punishment for the punishment? *Getting smoked.*

8

Cattle Truck

WE ARE HERE, AT THE PART YOU'VE ALL BEEN waiting for — the slaughter. Enjoy my torment.

The time had come to leave the safe confines of purgatory, better known as in-processing, and head to the better confines of just straight up HELL! As we waited for our transport to come, we gathered in bunches to gossip about what was about to go down. Malachi, who was the wise old sage of the group, but was only two years older than most of us at 19, had a soothing presence about him. His words were like gospel to the little congregation gathered around him, consisting of Achee, Brownlow, the Thompsons, Tia and me. He told us tales of what he knew, and it didn't seem that bad. A little screaming here and a little push-up there, easy peasy, lemon squeezy. Then you had Ross, a Jewish kid from upstate New York who was the pessimist of our group. He painted a slightly different picture of fire and brimstone, fallen angels, sodomizing and the works. He kept us balanced. Four silver cattle trucks stained with rust patches pulled up to the parking lot. The screeching of their brakes as they came to a halt echoed through the air and sobered us up to what was about to happen. One by one, we filed in with every piece of luggage that we brought with us, plus a duffel bag, the Chanel tote bag of the military. Once we were all in and the doors slammed, the voice of the army God yelled down, "KEEP YOUR HEADS DOWN IN THOSE DUFFEL BAGS AND SHUT UP!"

I hopped on board with my comrades and took one last glance at what now seemed like a paradise that I had not truly appreciated.

It was pitch black on board the vehicle and I was shaking like I was a four-year-old terrified of the dark. Every time anyone would utter a word, there was that voice again screaming, "SHUT UP!"

I had no sense of orientation, as it was so dark. I wanted to hold my hand up to my face, but I had so much gear, and plus we were told to keep our faces in our duffel bags. Can't break the rules, I thought. So I just stayed in the abyss, staving off the urge to scratch imaginary itches. The twitches always start with the nose and work their way down. Those were the tricks that your mind played on you in the dark, and the stress of this situation did not help either. The sounds of the tires meeting the gravel and the asphalt made for an excruciating sound on the eardrums. Mix in that the driver purposely hit every pothole he could find and you have a cauldron for a terrible brew of paranoia. The darkness was turning me into a maniac and a man on the brink of insanity. It didn't take much for me to reach that tipping point, but a rustle here, and a rustle there, and I couldn't help but think people were whispering to me. Now you might say that maybe someone was whispering to me, but the voices never said a thing, so this leads me to believe they were all made up. Being the obedient and terrified young man that I was, I refused to talk back and even had the nerve to try and shush the imaginary voices. Hypocrisy is a thing, though, and when I felt something drop from my bag, it made it even harder to ask for help to pick it up. I had been shushing the people next to me for I don't know, maybe thirty minutes, so I was first determined to reach for my lost item myself. I don't know why this item was so important to me. Hell, I didn't even know what dropped, but I know I needed it. I bent down to reach for it whilst still holding my duffel with one hand. The whole time I'm whispering, "Pardon me. Excuse me. Sorry, my bad." My head and hands brushed up against breasts, chests, asses and other unspeakable objects. Some of the things that happen in a cattle truck should stay in a cattle truck.

I had almost given up, but I was still obsessed in finding a piece of material that probably had no worth to me. So I gathered my pride and decided I had to do it. I whispered, "Hello, over there."

I tapped around on the shoulders of the poor souls that I had tormented with my accusations and groping, but of course, no one answered because I was a douche just seconds earlier. Still I was a man possessed and needed this damn thing, so I whispered a little louder, "Hey guys, can you help me?"

Instantly, a voice rebuked back, "SHUT UP AND KEEP THOSE HEADS IN YOUR DUFFEL BAGS!"

I knew that was coming, but I had come way too far to let God stop me now. At this point, I had abandoned my whisper voice and went all in on talking, "Can any of you guys help me pick up something I dropped?"

Immediately the voice struck back with, "That's it! I got something for you."

I heard him or her burrowing through the cattle. He, apparently, was getting closer with every grunt from the group and I had to move. I shimmied my way through the crowd, causing a wave of my own grunts. I couldn't see a thing but somehow, I don't know, his specialized army training kept him moving in my direction. I just had to keep moving until he gave up, and then I hit the wall, something that was bound to happen because this was a truck and not a pasture. I froze in place. My only hope now was to stay still and pray for a miracle. The still allowed me to hear everything happening around me. The heavy breaths, the thumping heartbeats, the clattering teeth and the droplets of nervous sweat on the metal floor. We were cattle and all being chased in different ways. Screech! The truck came to a sudden stop and like a broken needle on a record, the door opened wide. An avalanche of light stormed through. The bright light blinded the whole truck like a stun gun, including my pursuer. Eight silhouettes with brimmed hats and super-hero poses appeared faintly in the light. The shadows screamed one line that still haunts and pokes my memories daily, "Everyone get off my cattle truck!"

So I did, and you know what? The light doesn't always bring good sh!#.

9

Private Upchuck

A "SHAKEDOWN," ACCORDING TO *Merriam-Webster's Dictionary*, is defined as: "The act of taking something (such as money) from someone by using threats or deception."

The first day of Basic Training is no different. A shakedown is how the military inventories your packing list items in an amusing way. Your first day is the first of many in the process of breaking you down to build you back up. As soon as we darted from the cattle truck with our bags clutched to us like vests, the verbal bullets were spraying everywhere from those mysterious shadowy people.

With demands like, "You have ten seconds to get to my water tower, soldier," or my favorite, "You look torn up from the floor up. Run," they asked us to do the impossible. It's nowhere as dramatic as hitting the beach in Normandy, but dammit, to a new recruit facing adversity for the first time, it feels that way.

On a blazing Missouri day, their first insane request was for us to dash to a water tower about half a football field up a hill, with all our bags, in ten seconds. My first thought while I trundled through the grass was, *How hard would it have been to fill out a college application? I could've gotten into Bethune Cookman.*

I staggered back from my first trip to the water tower, panting and clasping my knees. Taking a second to breathe, I got my first real look at those shadowy people, and they were our drill sergeants. They were dressed in green, black and brown crisply pressed, camouflaged BDUs and forest green ten-gallon hats.

Like a swarm, they moved in unison picking off all the weak souls they spotted. I saw one recruit sit down on the run up to the hill and within seconds, he was surrounded beyond visibility. A second later when they disbanded, he had disappeared into nothing.

After a couple of laps back and forth to the water tower, the lead drill sergeant ordered us to line up in ranks of seven with all our bags in front of us. Beads of sweat dripped from my brow, half nerves and the other half just responding to the heat. He then asked us, what at the time I considered the dumbest request in the history of requests, "Please pull out a left-handed tooth brush in ten seconds."

Collectively, we all stared at our mountainous pile of bags and as we looked up, there went our ten seconds. Like a swarm of jackals to prey, they gathered upon us shouting, "Beat your face! Get down and push!"

Dropping down into the push-up position onto the steaming pebbles layering the hard Ft. Leonard Wood ground, you could ask yourself the million-dollar question, "Why the hell did I sign up?"

One second, we were tossing everything in our duffel bags to find one black boot strap, and the next second, dashing to the water tower. This cycle of impossible tasks resulting in grueling calisthenics continued for what seemed as long as the Jewish slaves walked the desert. Somehow, we were steadily getting our inventory done. We were halfway through our inventory list when I found out what the words "battle buddy" meant. Exhausted, my hands clasped my knees for emergency support, and my heavy pants were in rhythm with my accelerated heartbeat. The rest of my compadres were in the same boat, as we were the walking dead, dragging our feet all the while believing we were hustling to every task.

On the fourth go-around of trying to find the Army-issued grid squares we had received, I spotted to the side of me the scrawniest, sorriest excuse for a soldier. It was like finding a malnutritioned child at a spin class. His BDUs were four sizes too big for him, and his body had the physique of a two-year-old girl. I felt sorry for him at first and then I noticed that he was using the soldiers in front of him as cover. He shifted his bags right behind him like a crash pad. I shook my head, knowing exactly what he was going to do, and thought this brother was insane. I tried to mind my own business and go back to my ultra-fun exercising, but in the pit of my stomach, I knew this could only end badly. While all the drill sergeants were busy giving kind instructional help to soldiers in need, this dude took his opportunity. He looked right and then he looked left, gazing right into my eyes, and in slow motion, he fell backwards as if the Holy Spirit had just touched him. He was out cold, sprawled out for the world to see.

In a flash, I turned around and continued on with finishing the jumping-jacks exercise that the rest of the recruits were performing. It was like seeing a train wreck. I just couldn't look away, however. I couldn't look away for long and slowly my gaze crept back in his direction. He was lifeless and I couldn't help but feel sorry for him. I couldn't just leave him there to die, so I stopped and took a step in his direction. The moment I broke in his direction, he winked at me, and a millisecond after that the whole swarm of drill sergeants descended on our location, like the police to a wealthy neighborhood. Someone yelled, "That son of a bitch!"

I immediately jumped right back into doing jumping jacks, praying that they hadn't seen me. All the drills surrounded him like vultures on a carcass. Their facial expressions did not exhibit fear or concern for his inanimate body, but fury. They snatched his skinny ass up and placed him on his feet. He woke up instantaneously. It was a miracle, but not so much for Private Buttler. They peeled what little self-esteem he had left right out of his soul with an ass-chewing reminiscent of a lion greeting a gazelle. They had seen the whole thing transpire from the beginning, and his plan had failed, as I knew it would. The funny thing about Basic is that drills are never satisfied with just one ass to chew; they want two, three, hell, all the asses in the whole world. The ass that they were looking for, however, happened to be mine, as I was the closest in proximity to him.

A drill sergeant barked at me, "Recruit!"

I looked around sheepishly with a "Who? Me?" expression on my dumb, green face.

He shouted even louder this time, "Soldier, as his battle buddy, how did you let him fail in such a spectacular manner?"

I replied, "Oh, I'm not his battle buddy, Drill Sergeant. I never spoke to him before."

I thought I was off the hook with a clear-cut reply like that. This reply not only didn't get me off the hook, but also incensed the whole drill sergeant crew. Now incredibly, I found myself in more trouble than Buttler. In seconds, they split their forces and took up yelling at me as their new hobby.

"Son, are you calling me a liar?"

For future soldiers, this is an impossible question to answer and you are better off playing dead than answering. I, unfortunately, did not have this advice and retorted, "No!"

After which they collectively responded with, "No one asked you to talk back!"

See, an impossible situation. I now, just like Private Buttler, was on the map, and they worked us over for ten minutes straight, making us do "up downs," "cross country skiers" and "front, back, goes" non-stop. They must've gotten bored or there just wasn't any meat left to pick off of us, because without any warning or signal, they all wandered off returning to the inventory.

With the drill sergeants gone now, I expected Buttler to say sorry as we picked our behinds off the ground. NO! That fool not only didn't say sorry, but he also went right back to the most failed boot-camp plan in the history of failed boot-camp plans. One duffel at a time, he relocated to his rear as his padding. This time I had to say something since now, in the eyes of the drills, we were spiritually joined. I turned to him and began to utter some words, but before I could say anything, he turned towards me and, absent of a wink facially, told me, "This is all I have."

I saw his body fall lifeless in slow motion to the Leonard Wood grass. As his body hit, there were ten drill sergeants surrounding us. I say us because they did not wait to bundle us up as if we were a crime syndicate this time. They snatched him up again and this time, ten of them got an inch from his face, barking at him. I almost felt sorry for him, but guess what? The other ten were paying me a visit. My head swiveled to all sides as I tried to keep track of the insults. I also had to contend with the other eyes from my new co-workers as I was thoroughly being attacked.

That's when I heard a loud *blurp!* Those Drills have the reflexes of ninjas because somehow they dodged the explosion of fluorescent green barf that suddenly exploded from Buttler's mouth. The vomit was on his bag and boots. Everyone paused in disbelief and when I say everyone, I mean everyone. The other recruits looked like wildebeests seeing one of their own get slaughtered. The drills, on the other hand, were oddly shocked that so much toxin came out of such a skinny body. I let out a sigh in relief that they had finally forgotten about me.

When the surprise wore off, the drills made him move three feet away from ground zero, and then smoked (exercises given to a soldier in anger) the heck out of him. The lead drill then called the whole camp together and made a declaration. He proclaimed loudly, "This soldier, Private Buttler, will from here on out be known as Private Upchuck."

No one chuckled outwardly but their faces looked amused with restrained smirks. *I was out of the woods*, I realized. *I made it. My anonymity had been restored. Yeah!*

The lead Drill, however, was not done. He made one more proclamation: "I was just about to blow the whistle on shakedown, but thanks to Private Upchuck and his battle buddy, Private Saleem, we will continue for a little longer."

If I wasn't hated before, I was now, as every recruit paused to look at me and imagine my death. I stood there shaking my head and thinking *if I had only gone to college, life would be different.* I could've been getting mediocre grades and failing at sleeping with college women. I definitely would not be dealing with Private Upchuck. I guess location and timing is everything, even in a jacked-up situation involving vomit and angry drill sergeants. *My life — I had chosen it.*

10

Battle Buddy Saadique

ROOMMATES CAN BE A CRAPSHOOT, especially in Basic. We were in the new Army and we had eight-man bay rooms, and let me tell you, my room was the sh!#! Not because of scenery or anything, but because of the six dudes in there, minus one, but I will get to that in a bit.

We had an assortment of characters in my room. There was Tolzin, the mellow Samoan who wouldn't hurt a fly but was strong enough to kill a bear. Next up, we had Walker, the corn-fed ex-footballer from Idaho who was more of a philosopher than a jock. Then we had Rosen, the cynical Jew from New York City. If you were ultra-optimistic about an event coming up, he'd bring you back down to Earth. Next to him we had Ross, a simple guy from the Midwest who enjoyed drama like people enjoyed gargling with nails. He was the physical embodiment of

Switzerland. I also lucked out and got paired up with my friends Malachi and Henry Thompson from in-processing. I got along really well with both of them. Henry was a slick speedster from South Cackalacky who kept your spirit up on the darkest day. Malachi was our fearless leader from Pennsylvania and the strongest of us. If you were going into battle, Malachi would be the man to lead you across the threshold.

Our room would be comparable to *The Avengers* in my completely objective opinion. I did say an eight-man bay, didn't I? *Ugh.* The last dude made my experience in the beginning of Basic a living hell, on top of the drill sergeants. "Sadie" was our "fifth Beatle." He was a mid-thirties Egyptian who was also the other Muslim in the room. As we got acquainted, Saadique heard my name and like a sleuth detective, he put two and two together. I should have said Bill because that was the beginning of a relationship that would take all my willpower not to fight head on. When the pleasantries were over, I threw my duffel on the bottom bunk mattress.

"Saleem, that is mine," a deep Egyptian voice commanded. I turned to see if he was talking to me and, lo and behold, leaning there against the wall locker with a smug deadpan face, Saadique raised his eyebrows and gestured towards the bottom bunk. My eyes flashed back to the bunk and, like magic, my belongings were on the top bunk. I gritted my teeth and smiled. To avoid losing my temper, my passive-aggressive superpower took over and I ate that slap in the face like the good little soldier that I was. Saadique rationalized it as, "I am older, my brother, and it is the Muslim way to share."

The author *(left)* and Henry Thompson during P.T.

If I had met a Mormon that day, I might have sold out my beliefs because I was convinced Allah was punishing me. This sort of behavior went on for weeks and as the drill sergeants let up and gave us more privileges, mine were being taken away one by one. Privileges taken away, courtesy of battle buddy Saadique included:

-I wasn't allowed to come in the room with my boots.
-I was given crap for not cutting my fingernails when they reached a certain length.
-I wasn't allowed to swear, even the soft stuff like damn and ass.

I know you are thinking if I acted like a chump, I might as well be treated as one. But I just want you to think of a seventeen-year-old with Catholic guilt and just replace the religion with Islam. I was a wreck because this guy was as strict a Muslim as I should have been.

As the first week bled into the second, I began to embrace his ways, similar to Stockholm syndrome. We were two peas in the same pod. We ate together, stood in the same platoon squad file together and shared a wall locker together. I couldn't move without Saadique. I smiled outwardly but was miserable inside.

This had to end. I was no longer going to be his lackey. We were in our stairwell after a long physical training, or PT, run, surrounded by all the guys when Saadique yanked my shoulder and stopped me. He barked at me, "Saleem, take your shoes off when you enter the building."

Every guy halted when they heard him yell at me. We were now living my nightmare, a captive audience to my humiliation. All of my previous subservient behaviors were confined to the safe havens of our room, but Saadique had now made it public. I had to man up now or forever be his whipping boy. I replied in my best rebel voice, "I know you ain't talking to me, son."

The crowd just got a little more intrigued and they began closing ranks and circling us. Saadique said, "Saleem, what is wrong with you? I am only trying to help. Now take your shoes off!"

The crowd broke into oohs and aahs, as if we were in a high school hallway skirmish.

Now it was my turn and I had to show I wasn't no punk,

so I said, "Why don't you take your old ass upstairs and put them away for me," and then I took off my shoes and held them out for him. The crowded hallway erupted into laughter, but Saadique's facial expression remained stoic and he gazed at me with judgmental eyes. I, too, stood frozen, knowing those words were not really me, but they did represent pent-up feelings of anger.

The guys in the hall patted me on the back, and for that brief moment, I restored some dignity. Saadique never hung his head, though he passed me on his way up to the room without making eye contact with me. I remember feeling empty but proud. I know those two do not equal shame, but I felt a little of that too.

That night, after a grueling day of torture, lights were out and I lay on top of my bunk staring at the ceiling, because that's pretty much all my body would allow. I heard a couple of faint sniffles coming from below, and mustering up all willpower I still had to move my body, I angled my head down on the other side. Saadique's back was turned from me as he looked at some pictures with his flashlight. Tears dripped on pictures of a woman with two toddlers. All this time I had no idea. I lifted my head back up and stared aimlessly at the ceiling again. I had to do what I did for my own preservation with Saadique, but I also could have done it with class.

He wasn't a monster, just another soul far away from everything he knows. I must've been the closest thing to normality that he knew and he tried to use me to center him. His methods weren't the best, but I was at blame too and could now see that.

The next morning while everyone ran down for formation, I had a quick second to talk to Saadique. He was a little standoffish at first and stayed at arm's distance.

He said, "Saleem, I get it. We are not friends. I need to go downstairs." I tried to put him at ease by replying, "Just hold up. I just need a sec."

He crossed his arms, prepared to give me no longer than a sec. So I had to move fast. "Saadique, I had no choice. You kept on making me do things I didn't really want to do." He replied, "I was helping you."

This prompted me to say, "That's just it. I didn't need to be helped. It's hard enough being chastised by the drill sergeants without having another overseer bearing down on me."

He relaxed his arms and welcomed in my words. He replied, "You could've just told me that." And I retorted, "You're right, but you are the way you are and I am the way I am. I only know certain roads to get to a destination."

I extended my hand and said, "I'm cool if you're cool, but things have to change."

Saadique looked at my hand, smiled…and clutched me in a bear hug. To the outside, it might have appeared he was attacking me, but Saadique was a physical type of fella. Although I wanted to believe things were all fixed after that, we were both works in progress.

11

Bunk Check

THERE SHOULD BE A BOOK CALLED *Soldiers Are from Mars, Civilians Are from Venus* because I had no idea what the hell my drill sergeants were talking about the first couple of weeks of Basic Training. We all had to learn a whole new culture, and fast. This culture included a few little learning points such as:

-How to talk
-How to walk
-What to wear
-How to groom
-How fast I should eat
-When to wake
-What to think

It also extended to how my bed should be made. I am not what you would describe as a quick learner—a moderately deep thinker and a catch-on-eventually type of guy, yes, but not quick whatsoever. Learning how to make my bunk was easily one of the hardest things I had to accomplish. Our mini lesson on bunk-making came immediately. They pulled us in our sterile bay area room and handed us the tools to make our bed. They weren't Italy's finest linens but rather a set of three sheets: a fitted sheet, a top sheet and the greenest, roughest blanket that would cut your face if you snuggled up to its front. Tossing the three-piece set in my arms, I had finally figured out that the texture of the sheets was the secret to the military's ability to wake up early. *Who would want to sleep on this crap?* After we inventoried our tools, we received a step-by-step tutorial on the standard procedure. The way in which the Drills talked up this process, it felt like it was supposed to be a work of art. It also felt like reason #3,043 why I might not make it through Basic alive. The Drills were pretty vague on how they wanted these bunks to be made when they explained it to us.

"Step one, place the fitted and pull tightly to get the wrinkles out."

"Step two, place the flat sheet down even on both sides, tuck, fold, tuck, and fold again."

"Step three, lay the blanket down tuck, fold, tuck, fold forty-five degree angle, and tuck again.

The actual tutorial was given at warp speed and without the opportunity to ask questions.

One Drill slapped down the fitted sheet and all four corners slid on like a glove. It was the first time I'd ever seen that. Another Drill jumped in and laid the flat sheet down. He might as well have been making a burrito as he tossed, flipped, and folded that top sheet. The third Drill had the hardest job as she had to make the Brillo pad of blankets conform to the curvature of the bed. She even bragged and said, "Who thinks I can't do this in thirty seconds?"

Afraid to raise our hands, we didn't challenge her abilities. She asked again, but this time with more bass in her voice. "I asked, who thinks I can't do this in 30 seconds?" We all raised our hands this time, strictly out of fear, not really believing she couldn't do it. She smiled and retorted, "Oh, that many of you don't think I can do it, huh? Well if I do, you all owe me fifty."

All our heads dropped, pushed into a bet we never wanted in the first place. She lined up next to the edge of the bed and said, "Say go whenever you're ready." We looked around at a room full of scared faces and collectively screamed, "Go!"

She was off like lightning, folding and tucking, folding and tucking. She might as well have been a blur. Not even breaking a sweat, she tucked the bed in and it only took twenty seconds. Sure enough, she turned around and said, "Half right face!"

Just like that we dropped to the floor and began pushing fifty. While our arms were shaking, straining to knock out our push-ups, one of the drill sergeants pulled out a dime from his pocket. He told us to look up. From two feet above the covers, he dropped it and the dime bounced back up. My face was caught in between agony and amazement while I was shaking, about to go into muscle failure. I so hoped this was not the test for the gold standard. Then one of the Drills said, "This is the gold standard test."

I was so screwed.

A drill then said, "You have one hour to practice and make your bed for the day. After that we move out, and it would behoove you to make them right."

The drills left us there to figure out the ancient military secrets of bed making. I had never heard this word *behoove* before, but it frightened the heck out of me. I turned to Malachi and said, "What does behoove mean?"

He replied, "To make your bed perfectly."

He walked to his bed and I walked to mine. It took me forever and a day just to fold one crease. Everyone in the room took pity on me and one by one, they showed me over and over again. I practiced that whole morning. By the time the hour was up, I got it, sort of. We stood to the front and scanned the room, looking at our bunks. We went from left to right. Each bunk was looking pristine, and then they got to mine. The room screamed, "Damn!"

If only they were saying damn because it was a work of genius; but no, it was because it was awful. The gang quickly ran over to my bunk and tried to help me salvage it. We didn't have much time, tightening in some places and smoothing it in others. A large rush of people outside ran past us on their way to formation and that was our sign to leave. We stepped back to take a last look at my bunk and thought we had pulled off the impossible. It looked like the rest. High- fives flew all around and we, too, proceeded to dash to formation. I never felt closer to this group that rallied, instead of crumbling, when a man was down. Teamwork surely makes the crease work … on a bed.

Later on that day, all four platoons marched back to the barracks from their training lesson. We came upon a horrific sight. Just the thought of it still curdles my blood. There was carnage everywhere!

The bed mattresses were stripped down naked. Single white sheets were spread eagle in the blazing sun. The green blankets were dirt soiled. What happened next was probably the worst part. The perpetrators of the crime strolled out of the barracks in slow motion, action-flick style. They could have been carrying clubbed baby seals because they couldn't get any lower. It felt like I had been bombed and I could do nothing but stare, as my body couldn't move and the sound around me had been turned off. The nerve of these jerks. Didn't they know we put our souls into those bunks? It took a little while for the shock to wear off and logic to creep back in, but I started counting up the mattresses and linens on the ground. The numbers, no matter how many times I crunched them, didn't add up to the amount of bodies in the company. No, by my math there were only a lucky few selected for this display, and deep down inside I knew one of them was me. I straightened up as I saw one of the Drills walk up to speak and thought maybe this was all a misunderstanding. He opened the dialogue with, "You are all pathetic."

Nothing good ever started with the word pathetic. He went on to say, "A couple of your battle buddies decided to make their bunks up like a soup sandwich. And now we have decided to start over and give them another chance to make it right."

I thought that was nice of them at least. It could be worse. He proceeded to say, "They will have ten minutes to remake their bunks and while they're doing that, you will remain in the push-up position."

It just got worse. If you have never had three-hundred eyes focused on you in utter hatred and wanting to tear your limbs off, you should definitely try it because it's invigorating. Not.

I now had to take my mattress upstairs with all my linens and turn my bunk into perfection when it took me literally one hour this morning with help. Sounds doable, right? The drill looked at his watch and said, "Go!"

As I took off, all I could see in my wake was a sea of my brethren drop into the front, lean and rest position. Their hopes and dreams now rested on us fixing our bunks. I swooped up my sheets and mattress with a newfound vigor and headed towards my barracks room, determined to help my fellow man and woman. Dashing upstairs as fast as I could with a full mattress and sheets, I got into my room and saw the vandalism was only contained to my bunk. I plopped my mattress on top of its springs and went to work. The clock was ticking and I had seven minutes left. I tossed the fitted sheet over the top of the mattress and leapt on top of it to hold it in place. I made quick work of it and moved onto the other flat sheet. Once

4th Platoon—Dog Pound.

I laid that one out, I remembered I had to lay the green one on top because they paired together. The clock read five minutes left. I slid from side to side folding at a forty-five-degree angle, smoothing and tucking both sheets under at the same time. I could hear the second hand of the clock tick. I had two steps left with two minutes and thirty seconds to do it in.

I grabbed my pillow off the ground, shook it and folded the excess material before placing it at the head. There was a minute and thirty seconds left when I just had the dust cover to put on, but where was the dust cover? I scanned the room quickly and found it on top of my wall locker. Those scoundrels! The clock read one minute left. I draped it over the pillow and moved my hands like nobody's business as I tucked that cover tightly in. Thirty seconds were left on the clock. I swept my hands over the top real quick for the wrinkles and then glanced up at the clock, now at fifteen seconds. I darted out the room and into the hallway. Out of control, I slid into every wall with every corner I took on my way down. I got to the stairs and took them all with one bound. The door was in front and my internal clock was saying I had three seconds to get back in formation. I bolted through the door to the blinding light, but could barely make out my formation. As I dashed with my last steps to my squad, the lead drill sergeant said, "Company, attention!"

I just made it and it took everything in me not to collapse or pant as I stood tall. My body was on the verge of collapsing as the lead drill yelled, "At ease!"

My body folded up like a lawn chair and needed Malachi to hold me up. The drill sergeants went upstairs leaving us to wonder our fates. While in formation, I looked around at the faces of my platoon with their legs wobbled and their backs slightly hunched, struggling to stand completely upright. To think that the inspection results could actually break them was mortifying because I was partially to blame. I needed this result to go my way. The drill sergeants strolled out the building without a care in the world, knowing their asses weren't on the line. I rooted my boots into the concrete, waiting for the results. The drill sergeants whispered into the lead drill's ear. I crossed my fingers and prayed for the best. I'd like to tell you this story ends well, but unfortunately, it does not. The lead drill screamed out, "It seems that your battle buddies said, 'Bung fung you,' and did a worse job than before. Now they have five minutes to redo their bunks. Half right face!"

The rest of the bunk derelicts and I ended up going back, not once, but three more times.

As for our fellow men and women, they got a little extra TLC, better known as smoking.

What I learned that day was, things don't always work out like a Disney film just because you have good intentions and motivation. You have to burn a little to get harder skin. The harder skin is also so the people angry at you for destroying their day can't draw blood.

12

Haircuts

FADE, TAPER, AND FLATTOPS ARE irrelevant words when it comes to getting a Basic Training haircut. I am an African-American male, and if you know anything about us, you know we are obsessed about our hair. We have an instruction manual on who can cut our hair and how, so a Basic Training haircut ranked pretty low on my overall memorable experience scale.

The line to the barbershop wrapped around the building two times and was as quiet as can be. The silence was like the calm before the storm. You could hear the mosquitos farting in the air. When I got to the front and stepped through those clear-glass double doors, it was like a Ford truck assembly line. Hair was flying everywhere! Four barbers stood behind four barber chairs, following one blueprint. Everything had to go. Females had to cut their hair to regulation length so it was always interesting to see the barbers' ears start to smoke when they had to deviate from the blueprint. Just taking a little off the back was not their strong point.

The emotion in the room varied. Most guys' faces were like, "Whatever, I knew this was coming." A lot of African-American males' faces were like, "This is not my barber! I want my barber!" Some female faces were like, "It's easier if I just chop it off." Then there was a small fraction of the female faces that were storming with tears over the loss of any hair.

When it was my turn to step up to the hatchet, I landed in my own special group. Just deaden yourself and let them murder you, because if looking like a clown was the worst you had to deal with, then you were winning.

13

First Sergeant Snur

THERE ARE PEOPLE IN THIS WORLD who, through situations in life, are transformed into miserable people. Then there are people who are just born miserable. First Sergeant Snur was one of those people. He was not much to look at. He stood five-foot-tall, weighed one hundred pounds soaking wet, but wore a scowl that would kill a man in his tracks, making 1SG Snur a cross between Yoda and Rambo.

Top Ten 1SG Snur Zingers:
10. Easy Peezy Japaneezy
9. Were you just born stupid or is it a talent?
8. The best part of you rolled down your mother's leg when you were born.
7. Why don't you just go ahead beat your face against the floor till you die.

6. Who in the hell do you think you are, the Pope?

5. You son of a bitch!

4. If I had a blow job for every time a soldier said that.

3. You're a total waste of space and universe.

2. Hey you P-R-I-V-A-T-E, yeah you, you ugly son of a bitch.

1. You know what you can have? A can of shut the hell up, that's what.

I recall during our first training lesson, we were outside and the steam radiated off the faded, black tar pavement, cooking us young, weary recruits like a skillet. I made the mistake of leaving my canteen resting on the ground, a rookie mistake. After sitting in the Missouri heat for what felt like an hour, I got a little parched and snatched the old green canister up to take a swig. It was like drinking lava mixed with lava. I gagged and wrinkled my face with every sip until I couldn't take it anymore and rested it back on the ground with dissatisfaction. I couldn't drink this mess, but I also knew I couldn't go up to the water buffalo (a giant steel water container) with a full canteen. So I looked left and right for the coast to be clear, and everybody was preoccupied with the training. I calmly reached behind me and poured the water on the asphalt. Within seconds it dried. Mission accomplished. I was good to get another refill. I coolly climbed to my feet and strolled over to the water buffalo with the swagger of a man smarter than everyone around him. First Sergeant Snur just so happened to be taking in our training session at that very time. I didn't notice that he was the gatekeeper of the water, so I didn't factor him into my plan. I reached for the spigot and before I could pump an ounce of water out, all I heard in this short, nasal, raspy voice was, "We both know, Saleem, what the hell you just did."

I replied in my best impersonation of stupid, "What do you mean, First Sergeant Snur?" I kept thinking in *my mind, He couldn't have seen that, no way, I was too careful.*

"Saleem, we both know what the hell you just did, pouring your water out when you thought God wasn't looking, but I was."

Sh!# was my only stream of thought as my mind had already built up how great that cool burst of H2O was gonna taste. I was a desperate man and had to tempt fate with a second sentence in a row to a drill sergeant. My voice cracked as I uttered out the words, "I know, First Sergeant, but I am really thirsty and my water was hot from the ground and I need ..."

What he said next shocked the hell out of me. His face softened, his demeanor changed and for that second when it was just me and him, he remembered what it was like to be a new recruit. He said, "No problem, Saleem. I understand."

I smiled with gratefulness but he wasn't finished. He shouted, "THAT YOU NEED A CAN OF SHUT THE HELL UP! Drop into the front lean and rest position and watch as all these soldiers who didn't pour out their perfectly good water drink."

As my hand sank into the prickly black rocks of the asphalt, I thought to myself, "Is God real and if so, why would he have put this asshole on his planet?" I pushed and pushed while one recruit after the other guzzled down water. The blazing sun was getting to me and the only thing I could do was accumulate the saliva in my mouth to moisten my chapped, white, dry lips. At one point, I began hallucinating and saw soldiers splashing water on each other and whipping their wet hair back and forth. I'm pretty sure I saw First Sergeant Snur taking water to the head with a funnel held by other soldiers, but I was pretty out of it at that point.

The whole while I just kept on pushing. My brain turned off and I was on straight autopilot. Up and down was the motion and the only thing keeping me going was the thought that maybe I'd get a cool, quenching taste of water. Seconds away from collapsing and my push-ups degenerating into the worm, First Sergeant Snur asked me to recover. He actually had to tell me three times, as I had resigned that I was gonna die in the front lean and rest position. I strained to straighten my body to attention. He placed me in parade rest and I kept thinking water. That was the loop in my head and the words coming out his mouth could've been Cantonese. My ears perked up and his words finally made sense when he picked up my canteen off the top of the water buffalo. Smirking as if he were the devil himself, he said, "Saleem, I took the liberty of filling your canteen up while you were resting. Here you go, enjoy."

He extended the canteen to me and like a pit bull to a bone, I nearly took his arm off. That's how fast I snatched it. I tore off the top and chugged it, and as fast as I did that, I spit it out. The jerk gave me water hotter than the lava I originally spit out. He stood there smirking from ear to ear. "Saleem, if you ever try and get one over on me or the Army again, I'll cut your nuts off. Now drink the rest of the water and get back in formation, you sorry son of a bitch!"

I inhaled the water in that second, lighting my esophagus on fire as it drained down. I dry-heaved a couple of times before scampering back to formation. I was pretty sure, though, I would never pour my water out again. That was the closest and most personal story I have from the Jedi Ranger, but one encounter was always one to many.

14

First Sergeant Snur:
Part Two

F IRST SERGEANT SNUR WAS MORE OF an embarrass-us-all than a village-type guy, an equal opportunity ass chewer. If you got out of line or broke the rules he'd jump on you, no favorites whatsoever. He hated everyone, but had a particular brand of hate for people he perceived as weak. His speech three weeks into Basic will forever solidify who and what 1SG Snur was about.

It had taken a while, but around week three you finally felt like you were getting your legs under you. You knew the routines: crap, shower, shave and make your bunk. The funny thing about getting into a groove is that life has a funny way of reminding you that life's not about grooves.

One morning, while waiting in PT formation and listening to roll, Chambers' name was called three times.

When a soldier was missing in Basic Training, nothing good ever came of it. The first thing asked was, "Who is Chambers' battle buddy?"

Once that was established, the following response would be, "Company attention! Half right face! Front lean and rest position! Move!"

Like I said, you'd get in a groove and know all the routines. Once that all fell into place, I waited face down in the push-up position for it to end. It usually didn't take long. A drill would run upstairs and then we'd find out a soldier overslept. A soldier would trundle his way to formation and we'd all go about our business. Well, this time it didn't quite go to script. A drill sergeant came out a second later, walked over to our head drill sergeant, whispered something in his ear and walked away. Before we knew it, the head drill called us to attention and there was still no missing soldier. This was odd but at least we weren't doing pushups anymore. We pushed out on our gingerly stroll none the wiser to what happened to Private Chambers. When we returned, however, whispers trickled through the platoon floors quickly that Chambers had tried to commit suicide.

Now it all made sense! The floor was abuzz. This was a scandal of the highest priority. I did not know Chambers that well, but she came from an ROTC background and was the daughter of soldiers. She was the type of kid that sang "The Star-Spangled Banner" at breakfast with her hand over her heart. It gave me pause to think, *If she couldn't do it then how the hell could I?* This was a premonition and reason #4,001 why I wasn't gonna make it out of Basic .

Within an hour of hearing the news, we were politely summoned to attend a courtesy formation with heckles of, "Get your asses downstairs in five mikes."

As we stood in our respective platoons, I glanced around to catch everyone's reaction and they varied. I had never known anyone who tried to commit suicide. I had seen a couple of after- school specials and they said there's no reason sometimes. I didn't think this fell into that category, considering I could see the reason with my two eyes walking in front of me. No after- school television program can prepare you for a person trying to make herself gone forever. This was serious. Even Rosen, our expert cynic, was lost for words. I stood there like the rest with this "Could this sh!# happen to me?" face. A hard expression to imagine, but it is the cousin to scared sh!#less. We were soon called to attention and then parade rest. This formation was clearly called for the Army's version of grief counseling. The person called upon to help us process this received his counseling degree from a little school known as HTHUU or Harden the Hell Up University.

Stepping out from the drill sergeant office with his signature stroll, which looked like a cross between a man with a stick up his ass and a gangster's bop, was none other than First Sergeant Snur, geared to help us cope. A man who always told it like it was did not mince words as he went straight for the jugular. In that raspy, nasal voice, he declared, "As many of you might know already, a recruit tried to commit suicide last night."

As I glanced around, the expression morphed from scared sh!#less to "Where the hell is this going?" As we stood in shock, 1SG Snur offered up his thoughts, "Yeah, a soldier attempted to commit suicide last night."

He lifted up his left arm and pointed to his wrist. "But see, you have to slice it right down along this vein if you want to do it right," he noted.

Those callous words drew a fleet of eyes popping out of our sockets. He took a slim, metal-fabric razor out of his top pocket and continued on with his soliloquy. "You also have to do better than a Bic razor. See, back in my day, when soldiers wanted to do something right, they did not leave it up to French-made products."

At this point, there wasn't a person at Basic who didn't think 1SG Snur was going to murder us in our sleep. He was cold, calculated and full of conviction. He finished his public service announcement with the simplest of messages: "If you are thinking of committing suicide, please do us all a favor and finish what you start."

Although we signed up, a majority of us couldn't fathom death. I know it sounds silly, but death isn't something the military puts in the brochures or on commercials. Chambers' attempt at suicide somehow made us question what our breaking point was if she tried to quit life within the first two weeks. First Sergeant Snur's speech did little to put our minds at ease and, honestly, at the age of seventeen, this was a little hard to hear. *What the hell had I signed up for?*

15

4th Platoon:
The Dog Pound

DRILL SERGEANTS ARE TASKED WITH the responsibility of taking a mere mortal and transforming him/her into a superhuman. This might seem like an exaggeration, but what the military stands for and what regular human beings actually are can often clash. The hardest part of it all is while they're being transformed, they must also try to become a team. This accomplishment is hard enough for the Justice League and the X-Men!

My platoon in Basic was called the "Dog Pound. We came up with that name as a team, but I promise you it wasn't unanimous. We were a motley crew, as most Basic Training platoons are in the beginning. All platoons were sectioned off in our building. There were also girls in our platoon, and I was reminded how lucky I was all the time by my infantry friends. The women were on the bottom floor, securely stashed away from us horny young men, or maybe it was the opposite way around and we were stashed away. To be honest, Basic is so grueling, women are the last thing on your mind. By last thing, I mean second thing, as two thoughts are all young males can have at a time.

Two fantastic drill sergeants—Drill Sergeant Mitchell and Drill Sergeant "Commando" Bauer—led the Dog Pound. Drill Sergeant Mitchell was the softer of the two, but being considered "nice" next to "Commando" is totally relative.

Drill Sergeant Mitchell was calculated in any decisions that she made. She only brought her temper out when she had to make a lasting point. For instance, I saw her tear an eight-inch-by-eight-inch hole through a private merely for bumping into her by accident and not saying excuse me. That soldier now has the best manners in all of the military.

Drill Sergeant Bauer, on the other hand, was who every guy wanted to be like. He was a true G.I. Joe. A former Ranger (bad ass elite fighting unit) and the unpredictable one of the duo because of his 0-to-60 personality, Drill Sergeant Bauer could be chill one second and Rambo the next.

The first time that we met our leaders, however, we were a little less than star struck with them. As the shock of shakedown was still fresh in our heads, we were cordially introduced to our drill sergeants in a tiny room. The room walls were a bland white and furnished with the same doo-doo brown wall lockers. These were the kind of colors that would implant thoughts of suicide.

They sat us down and gave us the rundown of how they run their ship. Their philosophy was simple. If we did everything right, this could be a smooth nine weeks for us. It was the kind of speech that gave you hope that there was still good in the world. Then there was a giggle in the back of the room. And you know the old saying, "This is why we can't have nice things." That totally applies here. Like Kang Lau from *Mortal Kombat*, Drill Sergeant Bauer flung his ten-gallon hat at the giggling soldier's head. The hat hit him so hard that in our eyes it took his head clean off. The private rubbed his forehead in embarrassment but the damage had been done.

Drill Sergeant Bauer leapt to his feet. By this point, he was actually green and his veins were popping out of his skin like an *anime* character. His next couple of words were like testament commandments as we heard them so many times over the duration of Basic. He shouted, "Platoon attention! Half right face! Get down in the pushup position! Begin!"

All over a giggle. That guy wasn't giggling anymore. The stares he received. The only person in the room that wasn't cursing him under his breath was God. No, he was mud. Our team was getting our first real test and we were flunking horribly. Ten minutes in and one female soldier, PFC Johnson, a tall African-American female and one of the highest-ranking recruits because of her ROTC time, had had enough. She halted all activity and crossed her arms as she stood in place, shooting eye missiles at our drill sergeants. Unlike all those SEAL movies you might have seen where people are allowed to ring a bell and quit, Basic is not quite like that. Drill Sergeant Mitchell and Bauer quickly barked out, "Soldier, you better beat your face!"

Then she said the unthinkable. "No!"

None of us broke stride from our cross-country skiers, but we did steal quick glances of this young woman posing there in her best F-U stance. I am not the smartest person in the world, but I knew this added up to trouble. Drill Sergeants Bauer and Mitchell smiled and commanded, "Halt! Side straddle hops (jumping jacks)! Start position! Move! In cadence! Start!" And then they left the room.

They were either master manipulators or just got bored. By this point, we were twenty minutes into our workout and without any supervision, we turned into pit bulls fighting for scraps. This was not a pretty sight, but what the Drills knew and we didn't was that peer pressure is the fire that forges a team into steel or pudding. They were banking on steel, I guess. One by one, we fell in line and jumped on her verbally. White, a sassy, mid-twenties, black woman, took the first shot. "Bitch, you better start moving before I whip your behind."

Then Brownlow chimed in, "Weren't you ROTC, Johnson? Come on, you know better."

Malachi, steaming, couldn't lay off adding his two cents. "Girl you better start moving them damn feet or I'm gonna make Basic a living hell for you!"

Even sweet, naive Sparks, from the depths of suburban Idaho, dropped in some bars. "How can you be so selfish? Start moving those limbs, girl."

She was catching heat from all directions. A surprising thing happened in the midst of the verbal ass-whooping we were disseminating. Our calisthenics form got stronger.

The whole room let their minds take over and we were hammering those jumping jacks out! We were moving like water, as my old kindergarten teacher would say. The drills returned in perfect celestial timing to see us in sync and killing it. Johnson's bad-ass stance softened when she saw that if she didn't get down with the program, she was going to get put down all by her lonesome. Like an old Ford pickup truck trying to get into gear, Johnson transitioned into her jumping jacks. Drill Sergeants Bauer and Mitchell didn't laugh or gloat but gave us the key to get out of the circle of exercises we were trapped in. Drill Sergeant Bauer said, "We will stop when you make this room sweat."

I won't lie. When he said that, it was as if the wind went out of our sails. Like, how the hell do you make a room sweat? Our BDUs were drenched as we were sweating from head to pinky toe, and we were all clinging to someone or something about to keel over. I did something very dangerous and let my mind drift in that second to thoughts of, "I wonder what my family are doing right about now?"

These are the type of thoughts that don't strengthen you but make you weaker. You can drive yourself crazy going there. I snapped out of it quickly when Drill Sergeant Mitchell screamed out, "Attention!"

It was show time. We had to connect the dots quickly or we would be here forever. At this point, I thought forever meant death. She screamed out, "Cross country skiers! In cadence! Exercise!"

Cross country skiers are the ski world version of air guitar. You hop around pumping your arms back and forth while simultaneously hopping and dragging that leg with you like skis. We were getting our fill of the slopes today, but I tell you, after forty minutes of pain on a black diamond hill, genius will be created. We figured out if we just built up enough condensation from our body heat, we could create precipitation on the walls of the room, causing it to sweat.

All of our heads bobbed, from eye contact to eye contact, becoming one collective brain. The decision was that for ten minutes, we would give it our all. And we did, turning up the heat and making every ugly, Rocky-workout face possible while doing it. We pumped out rep after rep of whatever silly exercises the Drills wanted until they finally shouted, "HALT!"

Drip drop, drip drop. Little droplets of water dropped on my face and on the faces of my comrades. Some of them even stuck their tongues out to drink the drops of water as if we were in the Sahara. The room was dead silent. We dared not cheer for victory, but the glimmer in our eyes was where the fireworks of celebration resided. Our drill sergeants said those magic words. "You are released for the night."

The rules of engagement had been laid down. We knew what was expected of a team and how to proceed further. As privates, we didn't save the world that day from Al Qaeda or Cobra Commander, but we moved in one direction for the first time. On the plus side, I learned a multitude of different exercises that day. But most importantly, I learned that, on my own, I could look really silly accomplishing very little. As part of a team, however, I could look really silly accomplishing the impossible. *Making a room sweat.*

16

First Call Home

SEVENTY-TWO HOURS WAS THE LIMIT of the law for how long the Army could keep you from talking to your loved ones back home. After straggling into the building with a rough day of training behind us, the powers that be decided to throw us a bone. They told us that we were allowed to call home. We had only been there three days but damn, I felt I had changed so much that I wondered if my family would recognize me.

As soon as they released us, I had a choice: dash downstairs along with the herd of my compatriots, or take a shower because I was funky as hell. I love my family, but shower time was at a premium and I really stank. After my shower, I strolled downstairs at my leisure, thinking that everyone would be on his way up by now. I was wrong. The line looped around the only two pay phones at our disposal. For you kids reading this book, when I went to Basic Training, it was before cell phones were the size of Lego pieces and accessible to the masses. We had an hour till we had to go upstairs and the line looked like it had two hours left in it. All I could do was pray for quick conversations and the Lord to strike some of these people dead. There had to be some really bad sinners amongst the group. While I waited, I sparked up conversations with a couple of my line mates. There was Sparks, from the middle-of-nowhere Idaho, who admittedly had never known a black person up until this point. She was not a racist by any stretch, just an honest girl leaving home for the first time like most of us. She might have been the sweetest person I met at Basic . Then there was Brownlow, a legacy soldier who had been raised for this since he was born. Legacy or no legacy, he still had the same crackle in his voice we all did when talking about our future at Basic .

There were also soldiers I met in line like Williams, who had the muscle mass of a pancake and looked like a teddy bear, leaving you to wonder how they were allowed to join the military, period. The thing with soldiers like that is if they make it past the first day, they will probably make it all the way to the end. She was full of smiles and giggles, ready to tell her parents, "I told you so," but in the nicest way.

Talking to people made me feel better and helped the time pass. The time passing quicker than the line moving began to be a problem though. I looked at my watch. I only had a half hour left and even though the line went from a double to a single file, I still needed a miracle. That miracle came in the form of Drill Sergeant Spike, the most questionable of all the Drills. He barked at his platoon to come over there for a violation. I can't even tell you what it was, but their vacancy spelled "win" for me. I danced down the path leading to the phones as they parted like a Soul Train line. I only had one person in front of me. With two pay phones and twenty-five minutes remaining, *I was gold*. Or at least I thought.

As one of the people on the pay phones got off, I was the next heir to the receiver. I was sitting pretty and ready for my turn. That is when things got a little bit too interesting for my taste. One minute passed, then five, and before I knew it, there were only fifteen minutes left.

You know, I wasn't totally sweating yet, hoping these guys would get off any second now.

I assessed the situation, analyzing the size of both people on the phone. One guy was this big Mexican fella with bulging biceps who was aggressively talking on the phone like it was a Spanish soap opera. The other was lily-white Sparks, sobbing on the phone to her mom as if she just found out her favorite pig on the farm died. I conducted a risk assessment as time ticked, and I needed to get one of them off the phone. I thought to myself, black male making lily-white female get off the phone as she is in full sobfest in Missouri equaled me appearing like the bad guy on a reality TV show. Down the other end of the barrel was an ass-whooping from my Latino brother who would make me look like one of Manny Pacquiao's opponents. I took another look at my wrist and realized that there were only seven minutes left. I tapped my Latin friend on the shoulder and squeaked, "Do you think I could jump on the phone before lights out?"

He turned around with a scowl that told me in my heart of hearts that I had made a serious error in my decision-making process. He opened his mouth and eloquently said, "No problem, brother," and then offered some other Spanish words to the phone. He hung up and smiled, saying, "All yours, brother."

I had six minutes remaining and I punched in my phone card code (handy for long distance). "Sorry that code is invalid," an automated voice shot back to me.

All kinds of four-letter words flew out of my mouth. I was so mad. I punched that code in about a billion more times, each time checking my watch. The sweat dangled from my brow like dreadlocks as the codes continued not to work, until there were only three minutes left. There weren't many soldiers behind me, but the few were looking at me with ill intent. I just stared back, like *you don't know the big Neanderthal I just throttled for this spot.* Frustration had finally overtaken me and I just said screw it, and dialed the operator. She calmly answered the phone, "Missouri operator line, how may I help you?"

I took a peek behind me and the soldiers that appeared a little peeved just a second ago, now looked ravenous with talons for fists. My voice was two decibels higher now and panicked. "I need to be patched into the Virgin Islands STAT!"

She replied, "Will that be British or U.S.?"

In a panic, I screamed at her, "U.S. for Pete's sakes, lady! I don't have much time!"

As she patched me into my call, I scanned down and had under three minutes now. *Ring! Ring! Ring!* I moved closer into the belly of the pay phone, searching for security as the line was moving in closer for blood. My youngest brother, Zayd, answered the phone and was asked the magic question, "Do you accept these charges from Khalid Saleem?"

I looked down at my watch and had two minutes left. Wondering what kind of substantial conversation I could still have, I did not know. My brother then had the nerve to say, "Um, I don't know."

With a clownish snicker humming across the phone, I belted out, "Stop playing around on the damn phone!"

He screamed out, "Mom, Khalid said a bad word on the phone!"

My mother snatched the phone from him and yelped, "Yes, we accept!"

I looked over and saw my drill sergeant gazing at his watch at the door. I had thirty seconds to make this memorable. I began to mutter some words, but before I could roll them out, my mom said, "I love you, baby!"

A deep voice jumped on and said, "Love you too, Khalid." Then my two brothers followed suit.

"Love you too, big head!" "Glad you're still alive!"

I beamed with the biggest smile and shot the people in line, who were still vexed with me, a goofy smile too. This phone call was like a battery charger for my spirit.

I looked down and I only had twenty seconds left by my watch before I had to run. Stammering, I mumbled out, "I love you guys! I know you don't think I can do this but I will. I hope at least."

Before my mom could get out another word, the drill sergeant gave the signal to hang up with a wave of the hand. I shot out, "I love you," and hung up. I walked back thinking to myself, it's not how much you say to the people you love, but that you say the words *I love you*. To my count, that was reason number one that I was gonna make it out alive, compared to the 3,048 reasons I was not. Trust me, that one is weighted differently where it counts.

17

Getting Smoked

W E HAVE ALREADY COVERED THE term "getting smoked," but I don't think I am doing it justice at all. Imagine your muscles quitting on you and then bitch slapping your mind into submission. Eventually, this leaves you a vegetable, drooling from your mouth and getting screamed at by people in uniforms. That said, I totally think I am still underselling it. A good smoking could happen anywhere:

-In a room
-On a field
-In a gym
-In a closet
-In the chow hall
-On a roof
-Outside a church (*inside* was frowned upon by God)

Well you get the point...

There was this place that the Drills took us to when they really wanted to send a message. It was a nasty place filled with red cake clay, pebbles in the shape of daggers and air as dense as lead. This vile place was called the "sand box," and it was located at Ft. Leonard Wood, Missouri, but it also exists in the corner of my nightmares. The first time in the box was always the worst. I can't even remember the reason we were there but I remember the long slow march from our company barracks. It was that cattle truck feeling all over again. The gases bubbled up inside your solar plexus and the pee built up in the place where pee builds up. We marched for what seemed like hours, but in all actuality, it was right around the corner. When we arrived, upon first sight, it looked like an open field house with dirt. I wished that's all it was. We would soon learn that it was a coffin of dirt and pollution. The Drills lined us all inside in rows of infinity and gave the command for the front lean and missionary position.

The fall towards the push-up position looked like an asteroid crashing into the Earth.

Boom! My hands met that rock-hard dirt with a thump that vibrated through my body. We started pushing and, within a few inhalations of the cloudy mass floating in the air, it drew thunderous coughs. I instantly thought this brownish cake dirt posing as soil could pose a problem if we were out here for a long stretch. Spoiler alert: we were out there for a long stretch.

One hour later, dust had filled the sky as if Harmatan had hopped over from West Africa and taken root in

Missouri. Our faces were a mess with grimaces of pain, camouflaged in dirt, combined with sweat and equaled, constipated mud faces all through the formation. The look on everyone's face was, *If I played dead right now, would they buy it?* I popped my head up from the pushup position, trying to locate Upchuck because he would have a plan for sure, but he was nowhere in sight. He probably found an out already. I usually have an optimistic outlook on life. If Godzilla were about to step on us, I'd think he'd pull up because he'd see that it was wrong. In this situation, however, it was hard thinking the rainstorm was about to end and a rainbow was on the horizon. Even I knew that the rainbow had been bogged down by the clay dirt.

That is when hope sprung up in the form of one of the dumbest plans ever. I say one, because there are many dumb ideas to unfold in this story. This plan, however, was the dumbest plan ever in the history of Basic Training. The plan kicked off like this. A soldier directly to my front started clutching his throat and gasping for air. He appeared to be faking by the floppy fish- like motions and distressed wild animal sounds that he was making. I shook my head, thinking for sure that this was the worst of ideas. Clearly his portrayal of a dying unicorn with all his "HEEA (*cough*) UGH" sounds would be seen right through and justice would be served. As the Drills walked over, I just knew this was Upchuck all over again. In the world of Basic Training, however, when you think you have it figured out, it reminds you that you know nothing. The fools helped him up and walked him to the side. My first thought was, *Are you freaking kidding me?* My second thought was, *If that were me, they'd be burying my soul and beating up my body to make my soul feel lucky.*

I, unfortunately, had a third thought which led to my undoing. I looked around and noticed that the Drills were as spry as when we first started and could do this all day. I had reached my breaking point and thought maybe things were different from in the beginning of Basic and I was the type of guy who could pull off this type of con now.

I pumped out a couple more push-ups and subsequently my courage. Like a sly dog looking for some scraps, I scanned the scene for my opportunity. Every drill sergeant was preoccupied monitoring a zone, so with one big gulp, I grabbed my neck and reached out for help like I couldn't breathe. I had to remember not to oversell it and give it a touch of Shakespeare. This was going to be my coming out party as the guy who didn't get the short end of the stick, but, in fact, used the whole stick to get what he wanted. What I wanted on this day was to get out of this sucky situation. All the drill sergeants dashed over to my aid. *The plan was working! It was really working!*

As I rolled on the once hard tundra, which was now my bed of victory roses, I peeked out through my fluttering eyes and I saw one, no two, no three other soldiers dropping to the ground and grabbing their throats. They were trying the same plan. My damn idea was going viral at the wrong time. The drill instructors who had rushed to my aid paused and took stock of what was happening.

I rolled, writhing in fake pain but pain all the same, as every recruit that fell to his fake asthma death became a dagger to my heart. Those same drills that were first coming to my aid snapped to their senses and were now coming for my lynching instead, for all of us phonies. The closest drill sergeant grabbed me by my collar, yanked me up to my feet and asked me a rhetorical question. He shouted, "Son, do you know that there are millions out there in America really suffering from asthma?"

At the time, he sounded pretty informative to me with information that I could heed for the future. I got it, punishment given and lesson learned. Now let's move forward. He didn't see it that way though. Instead he said, "Now get down and tell me how that dirt tastes."

I strained to knock out two push-ups before things got even worse. If being humiliated wasn't bad enough, the drill sergeants wanted the world to know that it was I who messed up. *Not the other twenty actors you caught. Just me!* The Drill added, "Thanks to your blue falcon soldier over here, this little party just got a little longer."

We stayed out there for an extra half hour, thanks to that flash of genius. By the time we finally ended, I forgot why we even were in trouble in the first place. I did learn another important life lesson that day. Shortcuts often lead to decision-making, good and bad. Boot camp was making me Confucius with all the hard-knock knowledge it was teaching me.

18

PT in the Morning

CRACKLE, *CRACKLE, CRACKLE* AS THE overhead speakers cleared their throats. I heard the familiar statement: "I'm proud to be an American because at least I know I'm free!"

Rise and shine! It's time for the day! That is how we started every morning. If you can believe it, "God Bless The U.S.A" is my favorite song to this day. Maybe waking up to this blaring over the loudspeakers every morning had something to do with it or maybe Lee Greenwood's sweet lyrics were the reason.

The morning routine was simple. Lift your head off your pillow, wipe the sleep out your eyes, sling your PT clothes on for physical training, decide between brushing your teeth or filling your canteen, and then sprint towards formation. You woke up at 4:00 a.m. after a sleep of roughly six hours to rush downstairs to work out. I guess the only silver lining in the sequence of those events was that I went to Basic in the summer months. Being warm and miserable beats the hell out of being frozen. PT awaited us downstairs every day at the same time every morning.

PT is an acquired taste that you hope to acquire sooner rather than later because the longer your body takes to adjust, the longer Basic feels. The first time I went to PT, I was terrified. I wasn't an ultra-fit person and made just enough push-ups to scoot on through to Basic . I was worried that I wasn't like any of the people in the Army commercials. Then I saw some of my comrades in action and, while I was not someone who could have been described as fit, I thought the Army must have really been hurting for recruits when seeing them. I looked like a decathlon Olympian compared to some of the other recruits. The calisthenics part of the workout further strengthened this belief. There were soldiers that couldn't complete twenty side-straddle hops (jumping jacks) or even stay in the push-up position. No, my first PT session resembled the "American Idol" auditions more than the "Be All You Can Be" ads on television. The thing is, you can fudge your way through the strength building part of PT, but the run was next and there was no fudging that beast.

We were all leveled off from raw data compiled during the processing phase. I also might be giving the military too much credit here. Somehow that raw data got me placed in the ultra- fast group. By physical appearance, sure, I looked like one of the speedsters in the outfit, but anyone familiar with me as a human being would know I might have been one of the slowest black men in the world. No, this wasn't the group for me and standing in that line amongst the other jack rabbits ready to sprint off their knees and stomach was a little jittery. The formation didn't take off immediately, and anchoring the left and right of me were two thoroughbreds itching to run. I stared at their faces, interested in what made them want to run for the sake of simply running. Their eyes were full of bloodlust and they had veins running down the top of their foreheads. I tried to engage the focused beast to my left in a conversation and said, "Hello."

I kept it simple because I didn't want to scare him, but nothing happened. I might as well have been dead to him as running was the only thing on his mind. Being an optimist, I turned to my right and said, "Good morning!"

This time my enthusiasm drew a response as he retorted, "You see me focused here, don't you? How am I supposed to run now that you took me out my groove? That was really selfish, brother."

And just like that, the conversation was over as I realized I was in a group of lunatics.

Besides, it was time to go since our drill sergeant gave the sign to take off. *Zoom!* The gazelles in this damn group they placed me in took off and left me standing there to ask that familiar question, "What the hell am I doing?"

I kept repeating to myself, *Just put one foot in front of the other and you should be fine.* About five minutes in, my legs were screaming back at me, *You asshole! Stop putting one of us forward!* I looked more like Phoebe Buffay from "Friends" than Usain Bolt at this point. All my limbs flailed like a newborn calf walking for the first time as I chased after my group. We ran for what seemed ages at speeds where the scenery turned into streams of light. I was hanging on but by a thread, as if I were on a treadmill at a level too high, and on the edge just trying my best not to fall off the machine. The thing about a treadmill, though, is that at least it will let you fall.

Every time I fell behind the group and felt like quitting, there was a drill sergeant screaming at me like a dog chomping at my ass to make me move faster. I was trapped and it appeared, even as fast as we were moving, we had taken the scenic route home.

By the time we ran back to the battalion, I was on my last leg and by last leg, I mean last body, as it jiggled and trembled up and down. My legs had mutinied and taken over as autopilot was in full command as I walked back towards our barracks. To my credit, or God's really, I did finish the run ages before the other groups and even got a bonus of being allowed to limp my tired ass upstairs. *Yay, me!*

After that first day of PT, most of my roommates were knackered and trying to find ways out of it. Reminiscent of a heist scene in a movie, we all huddled up to brainstorm. Malachi, our leader, noticed there were flaws in how they monitored the large amount of soldiers every morning. We largely outnumbered them and there were not enough eyes to go around. Malachi had enough and was ready to figure out a solution. That was when we saw Rosen stroll into the bay. He had a spring in his step and a beaming smile on his face. He might have even been humming a Disney tune when he tossed his reflective belt on his bunk. If looks could kill, Malachi, Thompson and I would have killed him with a stare. Rosen, who never got excited about anything, told tales of a leisurely stroll that the slow group took today, which was far from the reality I had encountered in the maniacal speedster group I was in. Thompson, who coincidently was in the same group as me but on the opposite end, had never seen me, as he too was focused on running as fast as he could, and he wanted out too. Thompson was fast enough to survive in the group, but smart enough to know that he'd rather coast. He noticed that they operated largely on an honor code when they asked everyone to find his running group. The honor code was our way in and the three of us knew it.

For the next three days, we cased the joint, observing every little detail about the PT routine. Our suspicions turned out to be true and the accountability was more myth than reality. By the third day, we were ready to make a move, but Malachi went far more left with his idea than we could ever imagine. He suggested that we skip out on PT all together. He had found a hiding spot he'd been using for the last couple of days. We were impressed because we didn't even know that he wasn't with us. We were so impressed that Thompson and I declined. The idea, as impressive as it was, seemed insane because the risk far outweighed the reward. Malachi had a set of balls on him back then that separated him from me. We split ways after that decision. Thompson and I had something less *Italian Job* and more *Great Muppet Caper* in mind, so we devised a simpler plan.

The next morning for PT, we went through our usual wake-up routine and ran down to the formation. We participated in the regular strengthening exercises — push-ups, side straddle hops and cross country skiers — just waiting for our opportunity. Then it came! The drills screamed, "Find your running groups!"

Thompson and I looked at each other, gave the nod, and then dashed to the slowest running group that we could find. We situated ourselves in the back like road guards. The road guards were the guys faster than everybody else and picked up stragglers at the rear of the formation. This was the best hustle in the Army, because you always had an excuse to slow down and you could stretch your legs. We worked our way into that slow group without a soul noticing us. *We made it!* This was the opposite of what I experienced before. This group was alive and friendly. There was talking and joking. Thompson and I turned towards each other, on the brink of crying. We knew we had found a home! The drills gave the signal to move out and, like a car with a bad wheel struggling to take off, we slowly moved into the road. Our kinda speed. We shot each other a quick five and took off.

Five minutes into the run, Thompson and I were

practically walking backwards in cruise control they were moving so slow. *Best plan ever!* Then the wheels fell off this Hooptie. One of the Drills yelled, "HALT!" It was as if a crazy switch flipped on the drill sergeant leading our formation and he exploded at the group. "What the hell are you all doing? You think this is some sort of hangout?"

Thompson and I looked at each other in the back of the formation and nodded our heads.

Yeah.

"Well it's not and, damn it, I have tried to be patient, but you all are saying bung fungo you to my kindness and I think I am a very kind man. What do you think? Am I a kind man?"

Without hesitation the group shouted back, "Of course, drill sergeant!"

Thompson and I shook our heads at this craziness, but still, we came from hell and weren't going to get too alarmed. The drill sergeant wasn't done and said, "I don't enjoy what I have to do next, but you'll thank me later."

Then he smoked all of us. It wasn't a long smoking, so Thompson and I weren't worried at all. That little meltdown should have been our red flag, however, that we had entered a new world of craziness. Shortly after, we stopped again for a short smoking, and again, and again until we were getting smoked every minute on the minute. Our twenty-minute run had hit the thirty-five-minute mark now and we were only a quarter of the way into the run. This plan had turned into a nightmare! We wanted out, but there was no way to get out. We couldn't tell the Drills that we had snuck into this group and we couldn't run away. We were trapped. The only thing we could do was run, get smoked, and run again until we got back to our battalion. So that was what we did. Thompson and I periodically looked at each other as the run and the punishment dragged on. We started out looking all spry and happy, but now our appearance was that of two runaway slaves fleeing the plantation.

Our PT tops were disheveled, saturated with sweat, and untucked. My reflective running belt was like a noose hanging off my neck and our pant legs had both risen to our knees. When that slow-ass train of a running formation pulled into the battalion, the sun was up and all the recruits had long been back.

There was one recruit who was not enjoying the sweet life along with us, and that was Malachi. He was having a conference with the Drills and the Sergeant Major in front of our building. Yep, it turned out that his plan had gone pear-shaped, too. He stared at the exhausted duo of Thompson and me, and we stared back at a humiliated strong leader in Malachi. There were no smiles, winks or head-nods exchanged. We all knew at that point, if we were gonna make it through Basic , it was gonna be the straight-up way and no shortcuts. I had just learned another life lesson taught by the good sponsors of Army Basic Training. When you set out to cut a corner, you sometimes find yourself running further than you initially intended.

19

Razor Bumps

THE *ELEPHANT MAN* WAS A 1980 film portraying the life of a young man stricken by a terrible disease that leaves him badly deformed. At times, I felt like the Elephant Man of Basic Training.

One of the key rules of the military is that you must shave. This was foreign to me as I could barely produce a soul patch or mustache whiskers in high school. My father didn't even have a chance to teach me about shaving as I was so barren. So the first time I shaved was in Basic with a Bic razor and Gillette shaving cream.

Are you familiar with what happens to a black man when a razor touches his face? It activates a countdown sequence that leads to a catastrophic event called "Ebola meets chicken pox." Two days after putting razor to skin, Pvt. Elephant Man was born, leaving my smile as the only thing recognizable about me. The thing about razor bumps is that they are ingrown hairs that don't just go away because you ignore them. Ingrown hairs just get bigger and bigger until they are unbearable giant tumors growing out of your face and neck. For the next two weeks, I walked around my company looking crazy with people grinning nervously in my face. I was the freak of Ft. Leonard Wood.

When I thought all hope was lost, a muscle-bound, African-American drill sergeant named Boon pulled me aside after he had seen enough. Sounding like actor Terry Crews, he said in this gruffy voice, "Soldier, get your life right! Walking around here looking all ate up and stuff. You have *pseudofolliculitis barbae* and you need to take care of that!"

Someone should have filmed us because the conversation quickly became a public service announcement for how people with *pseudofolliculitis barbae* should take care of themselves.

He continued barking at me a list of things I needed to do:

1. Go to sick call.
2. Get a shaving profile.
2. Get some hydrocortisone cream for that itch.
3. Buy some clippers.
4. Tell him if any of these other drill sergeants hassle me about shaving.

He did add one last piece of important advice. He looked me straight in the eye and slowed his speech down to say, "Under no circumstance, and I mean no circumstance, do you let them give you a yellow code tag."

I replied, "What is…"

And before I could get the words out, he snapped back, "Soldier, that is not important but what is, is I gave you an order! You'll know what the mark is when you see it, and then you deny it. As simple as that!"

And as quickly as the conversation began, it ended. He stomped off and I hurried to take Drill Sergeant Boon's advice. The first thing I did was go to sick call. Sick call is like the purgatory of military training bases. This is the place where all lost souls roamed, faces drained of all life, and you would see limp bodies indicating their time in Basic was done. Drill Sergeant Boon did not warn me about this desolate land.

I waited in this room, observing the faces of the zombies around me. Their eyes were vacant and conversation was minimal. The longer I stayed there, the more I could feel my ambitions draining away. Time moves differently in sick call. What seemed like hours actually turned out to be just minutes. When my name was finally called, I didn't know what time it was or what day it was. I quickly snapped out of the limbo trance after entering the doctor's office. He sat me down and gave me the rundown of the disease that I had. Maybe *pseudofolliculitis barbae* is not a registered disease, but it is a major "ouchie."

He said I was going to be all right, but I needed to carry around a document called a "profile" that let me grow out my beard an eighth of an inch. At that length, the doctor said all my issues would be alleviated. Then he rolled his chair over to his drawer and pulled out a yellow slip.

Alarms started blaring in my head screaming, "NO! NO! NO!" He turned to me and presented me with this tag and said, "You are going to need this tag to indicate that you have a profile. It's just a formality." On full alert I replied, "No, thank you, my drill sergeant said that I did not have to wear that and he was fully aware of my condition."

The doctor nodded and put the code back in his drawer. He then said I was free to go and I could pick up my hydrocortisone cream at the pharmacy up front. *Yay! I had been cured.* I marched out of that soul-draining slum and past all those desolate soldiers, praying I wouldn't have to return.

When I returned to my barracks, it was sometime around mid-morning and everyone was already at training. The drill sergeant allowed me to place my items upstairs and then come to training. I did a variation of his instructions and I dashed straight to the latrine. Like a kid with a new toy, I rifled through the bag of special cream and razors from the pharmacy. I popped open the cream, then took a look in the mirror one last time. The man staring back at me was an alien with boils on his face the size of craters. The medication instructed to use just a dab of cream on the affected areas, but a douse was certainly just as good as a dab, and look at me! This was an emergency. Glob, glob, glob. I drenched my face until

I was white faced. As I admired myself in the mirror and beamed with a grin at the prospect of being whole again, a drill sergeant entered the latrine. He exploded, screaming, "Soldier! What the hell do you find yourself doing?"

I popped to parade rest startled and replied, "Trying to fix *pseudofolliculitis barbae,* drill sergeant."

He smirked and replied, "Oh, is that all? Well, let's see if it is working."

The next thing I knew, he was dragging me downstairs in front of our barracks building where everyone was training. He pulled me out in front of the whole company and screamed, "Ladies and gentlemen, please don't come to attention. I actually want you to stay at rest so that you can marvel at this soldier. He is trying to end the disease known as…"

He gestured to me to finish the sentence and in a sheepish voice, I said, "*Pseudofolliculitis barbae.*"

At this point, with my face ghost white and body trembling, I was mortified and angry at the same time. I wanted to deck him as he continued on his rant: "That's right, *pseudofolliculitis barbae.* This brave soldier in his protest has painted his face white with hydrocortisone cream while you hard-working soldiers are out here training. So to assist him in bringing awareness to this cause, he will remain in parade rest in this fine Missouri sun until training is done or they find a cure."

As the drill sergeant left me to rot in humiliation in front of everybody, the whole company laughed at my predicament. My friends didn't mean to laugh, but it was hard not to at this tall black kid with his face painted like a Japanese geisha in skin-tight PT shorts standing in front of them. No, I understood. To their credit, they hid their snickers as much as they could.

About ten minutes into my stint, Drill Sergeant Boon popped his head out of the building and stared at me. I thought for a second, Hooray! I am saved! Instead, it was the type of uncomfortable stare that you give a stranger who just took a taste of your food without asking. Not the I'm-coming-to-save-your-ass stare I had hoped for. He nodded at me and then popped his head back in. I was out there for the long haul as the hydrocortisone cream dried my face and cracked. An hour passed and I was still up there. Parade rest is probably the worst of the positions, as you stand there with your arms interlaced behind your back centered at the waist.

You feel like your arms are gonna fall off and relieving the pain can only get you verbally slaughtered by the drill sergeants.

All the drill sergeants finally piled out the door and called the company to attention. I moved to go back to the formation, but the drill sergeant who punished me signaled for me to stay. They quickly moved the company out and left me in front of the building. However, Drill Sergeant Boon and the other drill sergeant, my tormentor, stayed behind. They both strolled over to me. As they approached, my heart beat a hundred miles per hour. I did not know what else I could have possibly done. They stopped in front and Drill Sergeant Boon shot a cold, hard stare. The other drill sergeant reluctantly turned towards me and mumbled, "At ease."

I released my stance and the weight slightly buckled me to the ground. The other Drill looked again towards Boon for what to say and then grimaced, eked out an awkward smile, and said, "I checked some facts and *pseudofolliculitis barbae* is a serious problem that I want you to take care of from now on. And if anyone gives you problems, please let me or Drill Sergeant Boon know. Now go upstairs and freshen up. Take an hour and then meet us at the chow hall."

The drill sergeant then shot both Drill Sergeant Boon and me a strained smile and departed. Drill Sergeant Boon angled towards me and nodded his head. He then marched off without even saying a word. He didn't need to say anything. I knew already that he had kept his word. Couple of days later, the bumps on my face had deflated and I was back to looking somewhat normal. All my razor bump problems for the rest of my career weren't solved with Drill Sergeant Boon's solutions, but as far as Basic was concerned, I was all smiles. This was largely because I had a guardian angel that could punk all the rest of the drill sergeants for me.

20

Blue Falcon

B LUE FALCON, AS DEFINED BY the *Urban Dictionary*, is a socially acceptable reference to the acronym "BF" — also known as "buddy fu@$" — referring to an action that leads to "fu@$-ing over" your "buddy." It is common in military parlance.

Here are a couple of examples of what Blue Falcon actions are:

-If you refuse to leave your bunk while your whole platoon is being smoked downstairs because of your actions, you might be a Blue Falcon.

-If you talk back to your drill sergeant while your platoon is in the front lean and rest position, you might be a Blue Falcon.

-If you refuse to wake up for fireguard while your tired battle buddy takes on another shift to cover for you, you might be a Blue Falcon.

I was in Basic Training with the poster child of the blue falcon society, Private Spruil. Private Spruil hailed from New York City and looked like the love child of Mr. Magoo and Sweet Brown. He also had the attitude of Fred Sanford. Spruil did not stay with our platoon long, but the four weeks he was with us felt like forever.

Private Spruil had a knack for getting under everyone's skin. He was rude, never punctual and had the fitness tenacity of a sloth. Most people have one or two redeeming qualities, but I don't know if he had any. I struggled to think of just one. Spruil was a late addition to our platoon and started at about Week 3. From the start, he was nothing but trouble. We were at

PT the morning after that fateful day, waiting in formation when he arrived. The drill sergeants conducted roll call on that day. As a platoon, we knew we just received a new soldier, but he had come in at night and we had not yet met him.

That morning, however, we got a 101 tutorial on the power of Spruil. Once it was our platoon's turn to give roll call, we counted up all the soldiers, remembering that our squad had grown by one and we were short one. The new guy had overslept. No big deal as we had all been there before, so my platoon sent me upstairs to fetch him. I sprinted upstairs and found the young man still curled up in bed. *Honest mistake. I'll just wake him up, we'll get smoked a little bit and he'll fall in line*, I thought. *Easy peezy!* So I shook him once. No response. I shook him twice. No response. The third time I shook him, he rolled over. I thought, *Are you freaking kidding me? This dude is in a coma and time was ticking.* This was an extraction mission and not a resuscitation.

I snatched the covers off of him and he woke right on up. I turned on the light and like a vampire, he shielded his eyes from the rays retreating to the shadows of the corner bunk. He snapped at me, "What's the deal, son!"

I snapped right back, "The deal, son, is it's time to go down to formation! Come on, you are mad late!"

He shook his head and curled back up mumbling, "I'm not going today."

I thought to myself this dude is insane, but time was up and I had to go back with a status update. I ran back downstairs solo to the alarmed eyes of my platoon. Drill Sergeant Bauer asked me, "Soldier, where is Private Spruil?"

Not really knowing how to tell him, I stuttered and replied, "Private Spruil told me to tell you guys that he didn't feel like coming into work today."

He flipped his lid. His hair turned bright yellow. An energy flame started reverberating off his body as veins I didn't know existed in a human being popped out of his skin. He was in full super-Saiyan mode. In his drunken anger, he placed a finger in the air as if it were a control measure for his anger and said, "Soldier, what room number is that idiot in?"

Holding back a smile, I replied proudly, "Room 238, Drill Sergeant!"

He was so upset, he turned to the head drill sergeant and said, "My platoon will stay with me for PT this morning. I got something special for them."

He dashed upstairs and left us in the front lean and rest as the rest of the platoons rolled out to conduct PT about five minutes later. Drill Sergeant Bauer came downstairs with Spruil in tow. I don't know what he said or did to him, but he was compliant for the rest of the morning. Yep, compliant, very compliant, as we got smoked from hell to high water. They put us through the ringer that morning, but when you looked over at Spruil to see if there was a drop of remorse in his face, there wasn't any. No! He was stoic and without an ounce of compassion. He might as well have been a sociopath. No, he was a blue falcon sociopath. That's the worst kind of sociopath. From that day, we knew we had been punished by the Army gods getting Spruil attached to our platoon. The worst thing about this story is that's not even the worst Spruil story.

My most memorable "worst Spruil moment" came at the most vulnerable moment for any new recruit, the gas chamber! The gas chamber is a small dark room where young recruits are ushered to and monitored by drill sergeants to see how quickly they can don their mask and protective gear before a hazardous gas consumes their lungs. In other words, a torture chamber filled with the exhaled regrets of young wanna-be soldiers asking, "Why again did I volunteer for this?" Some may think the gas chamber is that event in Basic Training where lore might outweigh the actual event. This is not true at all. That gas burns like holy hell! As a new recruit, I remember every recruit taking gas mask drills seriously, as if there were an imminent attack.

Every recruit, of course, except Spruil, as he never took anything too seriously, being from New York. He wore that New York attitude like a badge of honor. There was no one or no thing that would tell him what to do. This would not be his own undoing but ours.

Our platoon marched up to the gas chamber location, which was straight out of a *Friday the 13th* set. There was a lake, a creepy building and pine trees all over. *Yep, Friday the 13th all right.* We were organized in sets of fifteen and lined outside the chamber doors. The military is big on just hurry-up-and-wait as we stood out there forever. Lines of fifteen went in and lines of fifteen came out, all flapping like chickens with their heads cut off.

The best part is that once you gain your composure, that's when the real action starts. Your sinuses loosen up and the snot caps in your nose unfreeze and release. The rivers of snot roll down your lip, which by this time is quivering uncontrollably, and onto your clothes. Your eyes, which have been shut closed with tears, can finally open, only to now be hit with a blast of light that jerks you back, almost forcing you to your knees. Don't get me started on if you have to pee or take a dump. Let's just say it's not pretty. This was the signature gas chamber reaction that the drill sergeants treated like a rite of passage.

As it came up on my line's turn to go in, I looked down at our file, and lo and behold, Spruil was in it. *No!* I thought at that moment as I couldn't help but think of myself as a Biblical character going through a seemingly impossible trial. Of all the lines, why did this blue falcon have to walk into mine? I shook my head as they ushered us into the dark dim-lit room.

Behind a shield of glass, there were three drill sergeants accompanied by a plain-dressed soldier wearing headphones. I could see them staring at us as if we were cattle. We were sheep about to get slaughtered. The worst part of standing there is your nerves. If it were just my knees shaking, it wouldn't be that bad, but the goosebumps on my skin rose so high that they pulled my skin to the brink of coming off. Sweat flowed off my brow like the Yangtze River. I was a wreck, partially because of the uncertainty of the gas coming, but also because of the falcon amongst my flock. The silence in the room was deafening as no one was talking, even Spruil.

Then the voyeurs behind the glass broke their silence. Their directions over the loudspeakers smacked against the gritty black walls and echoed into our ears like nails on a chalkboard. The only word that came through clearly was, "Gas!"

The CS gas rushed into the room, much the same as missiles aimed directly at our lungs. As the gas bulldozed its way through the vents, and rose from my feet like rising water, I hurried to remember protocol. Step by step, I repeated to myself the procedures for donning a mask.

Step 1: Pull it out. That was easy.

Step 2: Press it against your face.

Step 3: Pull the harness over your head and fit the harness to your big head.

Step 4: Pull the hood over.

Step 5: Place your hand over the canister and blow.

Lo and behold, it was on in nine seconds. The room was infiltrated and filled to the ceiling with gas, but not one of my line mates was touched. The voices behind the glass then murmured through the intercom, "Now slowly break the seal of your mask."

We were halfway there and we were flying! My squad was killing all the commands so far, and all I had to do now was complete the breaking seal portion of it and I was done. *Easy peasy, lemon squeezy!* Wrong! Nothing is ever lemon squeezy with Spruil around, so when they commanded all of us to break the seals of our mask, guess who didn't do it?

What started as a record-setting pace by my line was quickly turning into the world record for holding your breath. The loudspeaker rustled to attention, but it was hard to hold your breath and concentrate on the words being said. "Soldier to the far left, please break your seal so that we can move on."

With my eyes shut, all I could hear was a resounding, "No!"

Spruil actually said no. *That jerk — sorry, that was an insult to all jerks — no, that blue falcon had taken it too far. He wanted us to die!* As I stood there with my eyes closed and holding my breath, I could feel my brain losing oxygen. What was once a tight seal was now slowly seeping in CS gas. The slow burn began at the tongue and then trampled down to the esophagus with the scorching of a lit match. As it skated down the esophagus and burst through the atrium door, it combusted in the lungs, feeling like a flock of flying and flaming razor blades lost in the dark bouncing of walls. This pain went on for what seemed like hours as the drill sergeants were in a standoff of screaming, "Break the seal!" Spruil barked back through his rubber mask with that cocky New York accent, "No! I ain't breaking this damn seal!"

Around the third cycle of this back-and-forth yelling, and I never understood why they just didn't yank his ass out of there, my brain shut off and I blanked out. To this day, the end of the gas chamber experience is still a mystery. I don't know how we even got out. For all I know, we actually didn't and we all died in that standoff between Spruil and the Drills. I could actually be writing this book as a ghost. What I do know about that day is we appeared on the other side of the gas door doing the chicken dance after being in there for record time.

Spruil's classic blue falcon move that day landed him in a heap of trouble. His actions also taught me an important lesson about how you punish a blue falcon. You simply let him be himself. We shunned him afterwards as we knew he did not have the group's best interest at heart. Living as a person who would betray the well-being of friends or family is punishment enough. A life lived without integrity is a lonesome one.

21

KP Duty

I OFTEN GET ASKED AS AN ADULT, "Why do you eat so fast?" My first answer always is that I grew up with four ravenous brothers, but my second answer is, you only need ten minutes to eat in a chow hall. The chow hall is cafeteria in military talk. You only went there twice a day, for breakfast and dinner, but they were two of the happiest points of your day. The chow hall came with a code of conduct that was followed by all—if they knew what was good for them.

Chow Hall Code Of Conduct

Code of Conduct # 1: No talking in line (outside or inside) in chow hall.

Code of Conduct # 2: Limit eye contact with other soldiers.

Code of Conduct # 3: Don't touch food that you would find in Willy Wonka's Factory.

Code of Conduct # 4: Say *please* and *thank* you to the chow hall staff.

Code of Conduct # 5: You have ten minutes to eat or else (the "or else" was never good!).

The exception to all these rules, however, was the weird paradoxical vortex known as KP (kitchen prep) duty. KP duty was the duty that you died to get on because you could get away from the daily stresses of seven fire-breathing drill sergeants, but this glory only came around once every blue moon. The powers that be rotated soldiers through all the battalions and platoons throughout Ft. Leonard Wood to make it a fair delight to all troops.

When the opportunity presented itself and the Drills asked for volunteers, my hand rocketed up. It was so high in the air I was like that kid in class who was dying to give the right answer. The drill sergeant looked around and picked everyone but me. He had chosen five soldiers and was down to his last pick. My arm was relentless and raised a foot higher in the air than anyone else, pleading for attention. He sighed with a silent reluctance, pointed in my direction and the KP duty was mine.

The next morning, instead of reporting to PT training or any other fun, torturous stuff, I was in a rotation loaded with six males as we marched down at dawn to the chow hall to report to the drill sergeant in charge. We were the luckiest soldiers in the world. That is until we saw who we were reporting to, Drill Sergeant Coleman.

Dun dun dun. She was the meanest drill in the whole company and standing at just four-foot tall, she glared up at us with her lips soaked in dark, red lipstick and froze us in place with fear. Her cheekbones were chiseled in just the right angles so that when you looked at her complete profile, she appeared to be an ornamental gnome sent by the Army to kill us.

She also was the only drill sergeant who had the trifecta complex. The trifecta complex is when three proverbial chips on a person's shoulders elevate a person's natural meanness to diabolical levels. Drill Sergeant Coleman was as short as a dwarf, female and African American. You have to work doubly hard when you are working in a tall, white, male environment such as the Basic Training world. Our platoon leaders also didn't do us any favors by sending six males over six-feet tall as a ceremonial offering to the goddess of jerkness. Her reputation did not fail her. The first time we met her, she ripped us a new one before even saying good morning, yelling, "Attention! Half right face! Get down, turds, and give me until I get tired!"

Yeah, she proceeded to smoke us just because we missed PT, something we had no control over. No, she was as mean as the devil and everything she was advertised as. A glorious day had just turned challenging.

As soon we entered the chow hall, she introduced us to a staff of sweet-looking grandmas. *Finally, a bright point.* I smiled at their friendly faces. They were like the Seven Dwarfs, though some were tall and some small. Their welcoming Midwest smiles warmed my jaded heart, but that was short-lived. Five minutes in and their smiles morphed into glares. It was almost as if Drill Sergeant Coleman transplanted her evilness into them. The old grannies immediately barked at us, "Get to work, you maggots! And take off those BDU tops. You won't be needing them."

For the record, three-and-a-half weeks in and this was the first time I had been called a maggot. These geezers had flipped their tops and began yelling out every cliché known to man while we prepped and ordered all the food in the chow hall. They were no longer the cuddly crew I first thought we were getting, but the geriatric witches of KP duty. The insults didn't stop, proceeding on with phrases such as, "Hurry up, Clementine!" and "How about you get that prance out your step and hurry over here!"

They worked us like slaves without a shred of breakfast. We scurried through that kitchen, jumping, leaping, sliding and diving, all the while sweating our asses off. At different points, those old sadistic witches sat back and watched us bend over, stretch, and even come in and out of the freezer with our t-shirts on. I guess that's why they had us take our tops off. Yep, we were definitely being mistreated and objectified, but we had a worse problem on our hands. All that parkour kitchen maneuvering took a toll on my body as the morning wore on, but I wasn't alone as we all visibly slowed our pace to a crawl. My arms trembled so much that I could barely lift a spoon. This was supposed to be the Valhalla of jobs, but it was turning into a version of Hell that was run by the Golden Girls.

The sun rose and the platoons started to roll in for breakfast. We had finished our work and thought we could relax. I should have learned by now that nothing goes that smoothly in Basic . We were assigned to serve our constituents. This was the lowest point of the day by far. As our buddies rolled through the chow hall, the code of conduct was the only thing saving us from verbal ridicule. The other recruits could not talk, but they could smirk, and their smirks spoke volumes.

We were in Hell while Drill Sergeant Coleman was smoking and joking with her friends at the Drill table. By the time all the soldiers vacated breakfast, we were slumped over the serving counters, propping ourselves up, trying to catch a breather, but knew the work wouldn't stop. We were pleasantly surprised when we heard, "Grab yourself something to eat and relax with some pop."

Pop was a term for soda in the fifties. I told you these women were old. Then we heard, "Good work!" We looked around to see where the voice came from, and it was Drill Sergeant Coleman. Our jaws nearly hit the floor. As astonished as we were, we did what the lady said. We piled our trays with grits, oatmeal, sausages, fruit and good old pop.

This job just went from sh!# to sugar in a matter of seconds. The group of us plopped our butts down and ate and talked and looked in each other's eyes just because we could. The party was on, that is, until Drill Sergeant Coleman came over and sat down. A hush blanketed the table, the smiles evaporated into thin air, and our love-lit eyes widened like saucers. We were terrified that we were going to get smoked for excessive happiness. With half-eaten food and crumbs around our mouths, we held our breath when she opened her mouth and said, "You know what's wrong with you recruits? You're too uptight."

We paused for a second, staring at her stoic face, but after a dazed moment of shock, both laughter and food exploded from our mouths. She sat with us and then spoke to us for an hour about the real Army life, training and life as a female soldier. She spoke to us about being a soldier and what you needed to do to survive. Drill Sergeant Coleman was human after all. We learned about the many awards she had accumulated while serving in Operation Desert Storm, how she was an honor guard member for the White House, and how nothing that is ever given to you is worth having. Hard work wasn't always my forte, but when I thought about all she had to go through and what having that trifecta chip on her shoulder really meant, it really hit home.

Drill Sergeant Coleman was actually a class act and okay in our books now. This routine of work hard and play hard went on for the rest of the day until we were released off duty at six o'clock.

The Missouri sun eventually set, illuminating the sky as we strolled out the chow hall with our bellies full. We waved goodbye to our seven not-so-sweet and slightly sexist granny wardens. One of them even winked at me upon leaving. The sad thing is I would have probably kissed her in secret if it meant an extra serving of chocolate cake. Drill Sergeant Coleman, being our supervisor for the day, had to march us back to our building. We couldn't help but feel a new sense of enlightenment for knowing one of our drill sergeants better. Drill Sergeant Coleman was our new BFF. *Life was going to be different now.*

As we approached our building, she commanded us to halt thirty yards away. This was the Mason-Dixon line and she wanted to say her last words and prep us on how we were supposed to treat our new BFF in public. You know the act. She looked at us sweetly with the grace of an angel and then said, "Half right face! Front lean and rest position! Move!"

Yeah, it's in her nature. Once a scorpion, always a scorpion, I thought. Things were different all right. She was meaner than ever. We never had a talk with her like that again, but it still warms my heart to think, we'll always have KP.

22

BRM
(Basic Rifle Marksmanship)

N INTENDO, X-BOX, AND A PLAYSTATION had been the extent of my shooting experience growing up as a kid, so you can imagine my anxiety when BRM (Basic Rifle Marksmanship) came around.

BRM is that time where you see the line in the dirt drawn between the suburban folks and the country, I-was-born-with-a-rifle-in-my-crib kinda folks. When we received our weapon for the first time — not *gun* but *rifle* — we were told what would happen if we lost it. *You might as well kill yourself because the alternative would be worse,* I thought.

Immediately upon receiving my fine military-issued M-16, A-1 rifle, I had to stave off the urge to pose like Rambo every five seconds. The surreal intoxication of handling a weapon for the first time was also quickly drummed out by the immediate marksmanship-for-dummies training that we were given. The great thing about learning to fire a weapon in the military was that they taught you everything you needed to know. I mean everything—from how to clean your weapon to the firing positions, from breathing when shooting to what part of your finger should squeeze the trigger. We didn't actually see a range for the first two days of being issued a weapon, but we believed we knew everything. I couldn't wait to go to the range and show off my stuff because in practice I was a stud!

Then we went to the range and our excitement was sucked out of us by its complete and utter lack of ambience. The range was a dreary place and absent any of the vibrant colors of nature. The gravel-paved roads were Army brown, the trees were a dull green, all the surrounding lumber was a doo-doo brown, and even the blue sky, if you looked long enough, had a hint of brown. The Army found a way to military-issue itself an Army version of Mother Nature.

Despite its lack of decor, this was where the real training started and we were given real bullets. And let me tell you, carrying around a loaded weapon is a scary thing.

The stress level amongst the Drills heightened when watching a load of amateurs carrying around loaded assault rifles. Every wrong twitch or deer-in-headlights look in your eye and you got an ass chewing. You were told to hold your weapon facing in the direction of the range, which is also known as "down range," and never at anyone. *Bullets or no bullets!* The drill sergeants had perfect reasons to be scared. My mother never even allowed me to have toy guns growing up. She would throw them out of the car window or in the trash. I think she would probably burn them on sight if they ever came inside my house. It wasn't like we were high-risk kids or anything, but guns were taboo in my childhood. So, yeah, my drill sergeants were wise to be a little skittish around me.

While I thought I was ready before I came out to the range, I now could barely walk with my weapon in hand as my hands vacillated so much. Teaching me the ways of living with a rifle was going to be a challenge and, even more so, getting my rifle and me to have a symbiotic relationship was going to be a Biblical feat.

In military movies, you might see them skip straight to the shooting phase of the weapon- user relationship. That is pure rubbish. Like any good relationship, you actually have to date your weapon. You have to get to know your weapon, court for a while, hold and caress your weapon, and then make it yours. Sounds easy, right? In my case, like all women I met, it was stubborn as hell and didn't want to be owned. I named my weapon Margarita, after my girl, but as hard- headed as she was, I knew this would be a challenge.

Our first date together had a vintage setting where the sunlight crept through the green pine trees, the gentle breeze pranced across the skin delivering little kisses, and the birds chirped sweet nothings in the air. The only damper was that the range was an older one with pop-up targets that resembled World War II battle-fatigued vets. There were large holes in the ground, eight-feet deep and walled with concrete called foxholes, used for standup shooting. They were the epitome of romantic—cold, clammy, dark and deep. The fields stretched for ages into the sun's horizon. A lovely place, if I do say so myself, and only the finest for my baby. The range was the first real quality time we spent with our new boo, aka M-16. We stared into its eyes while standing in firing order under the romantic, Army-issued green shrubbery. That is where we waited in silence wondering if we were going to have the guts to do something, kind of like an eighth-grade winter formal.

When a number was called, the Drills marched a recruit out across the edge of the safe part of the range where the gravel and shooter reside. I tapped Margarita in anticipation for our chaperone to show us to our room. By the time my drill sergeant finally came, I had practically gotten to first base with the amount of times I stroked Margarita, trying to control my nerves. My drill sergeant dropped us off at our respective foxholes, one by one. When he dropped us off by mine, I couldn't help but think, *What if I'm not good or can't perform?* After all, I was a virgin and had no idea what this woman wanted. We waited and waited in silence until a robotic but soothing voice streamed across the loudspeakers. "Are you ready to the left?"

A drill sergeant raised his paddle on the red side, indicating let's go. "Are you ready in the center?"

Again a quick wave of the paddle. "Are you ready on the right?"

One more wave of the magic paddle and, in the tradition of ring announcer Michael Buffer, the voice uttered what would soon be the magic words of the range. "Pick up your weapon and take up position in your foxhole-supported stance," the voice asserted. "Insert one fully loaded, twenty-round magazine and lock and load. Watch your lane and fire."

Bang! Bang! Bang! Pop-up target after pop-up target emerged from the ground and I shot at them. Unfortunately for me, none of them went down. I failed to knock down a single one. I was convinced that there were holes in them. When the firing ended, I had only managed to hit nine out of the total forty targets. My first date was a disaster, but with glass half full, at least I wasn't a virgin any longer.

On my second date, I wanted to look past my first rocky experience. There was a little tension after how bad I was the first time, but my rifle and I decided not to talk about it and look towards the future. We went through the same courting process as before and this time, as we were dropped in our foxhole, I was determined to make this date different. I went over in my head all the things that went wrong when I fired on the last go-around. The only reason I could attribute my failure to knock down the targets was a case of nerves. So I went through some breathing activities I had seen on TV and it seemed to work. I was in a good place and as the sultry voice was about to return any second, I was primed for redemption. I don't know what happened when Drill Sergeant Bauer said, "Soldier, pop your head up from your foxhole." And like an idiot, I said, "Yes, Drill Sergeant!"

The "Yes, Drill Sergeant" wasn't the problem, but pointing Margarita directly in his face with a loaded magazine was. This was an epic failure and equivalent to a father walking in on his daughter naked with a dude. Drill Sergeant Bauer yelled, "Soldier!"

I snapped to my senses and realized the gravity of what I had done, quickly angling the weapon away. He then bear-crawled over from the foxhole right next to me, snatched me out of my foxhole by my BDU collar and yelled, "You think this is a game! I take this seriously and every time some young idiot like you thinks this is a joke, I want to kill him!"

He held me suspended in air for what seemed an eternity. The others in nearby foxholes stared in our direction after popping their heads up from their holes in the ground like stunned gophers. The drill sergeant suddenly dropped me down and in a cool, calm voice said, "Saleem, let's look at your sight aperture."

As he inspected Margarita, I hesitantly eased my way back over to him and listened to his advice. Needless to say, that date was a total wash and snowballed the rest of the day of training. What made it worse was that the drill sergeants gathered all of us together and told us that those who did not qualify tomorrow would be recycled. Recycled meant that we would start Basic Training over in a new class. This was disastrous for me because for one, I wasn't mentally strong enough to start again, and two, it would prove everyone who doubted me was right. There was only one thing I could do, worry all night and pray to the NRA gods to provide a miracle.

The next day rolled around and this was my last chance to make a good impression on Margarita. It was qualifying day and the mood was perfect for redemption. The sun lit brightly in all the right spots, making the target field clear to see. The wind blew gently, cooling just enough so sweat wouldn't tumble in the eyes, The birds even chanted, "Get some!" ever so lightly as they hummed by my ears. Margarita and I were ushered back to a place we found to be the beginning of the end of a good day, the foxhole. We began in the supported shooting stance. I fixed my sandbags and pallets with perfect positioning. The robotic voice to put us in the mood came on across the loudspeakers one last time, almost as if he spoke to me. "Pick up your weapon and take up position in your foxhole-supported stance," he instructed. "Insert one fully loaded twenty-round magazine and lock and load. Watch your lane, Khalid, and fire."

Pow! Pow! Pow! The firing started as usual, but this time, in a twist of fate, I was hitting everything. I mean, I was on fire! By the time the voice from above asked for a cease fire, I had hit at least fifteen out of the first twenty possible shots. My confidence was riding high, as all I needed now was to hit eight out of the next twenty shots. *Easy peezy!* We moved into the prone unsupported and I prepped all of my sandbags to the perfect position. High on life at the moment that magical minstrel came over the P.A., I *knew* he was speaking to me this time.

"Pick up your weapon, you sexy man, Khalid, and take up a kick-ass position in your foxhole-supported stance. Insert one fully loaded twenty-round magazine, as if you need all of them, you animal, and lock and load. Watch your lane, K-Dog, and fire."

I was ready and I kept my hot streak going, hitting all of my first five targets. I was unstoppable, the famous last words of a very foolish boy. I went ice cold from there on out. I could not hit the broad side of a barn.

I was down to my last four targets, with my last three bullets, and needed just two for the win. I finally got off with a hit and had to be judicial with my last three targets. The next target popped up and it was the 250-meter one, the target you go for because it looks easy, but it's not. I knew that psychologically this was the one you underestimate and you end up missing by the slightest. I passed that one up and waited for the next one that turned out to be the fifty-meter target. *Thank you, Lord!* I had nailed all my fifties to this point and this would be no different.

Bang!
Miss!
No!

I was devastated and down to my lone bullet and with my luck, the next one would be the furthest target, the 350. My luck struck again and it was a 350. Hitting the 350 target is like picking off a star out in space with a slingshot. I was doomed. There was no time to feel sorry for myself. I ran through the training in my head like a 1980s movie montage. In slow motion, I checked my breathing, posture, finger position and squeeze.

Bang!

The bullet darted across the arid terrain, past the dirt mounds, and then *ping*. That 350 appeared to be a million miles away, and slowly tumbled over. The only problem was that I couldn't tell if I hit it or if it was on its natural retraction back to the rest position. I had to wait for the scores to come from the voice above. Five minutes of agony passed when the voice returned. I waited through ten other soldiers' scores until it got to mine when he said, "Lane number 16, you beast of a man, you hit twenty-three out of forty targets."

Okay, maybe he didn't say "beast," but he did say I qualified. Margarita and I stared at each other under the pine tree, engaged in our post lovemaking cuddle, smiling at each other. I had survived BRM, won my rifle's heart and earned the title of marksman. I learned that day that fear is a great motivator if you let it work for you and not against you.

23

Phases

THERE ARE THREE FLAGS YOU AIM TO attain during your time in Basic:

-Red Flag — *Patriot*
-White Flag — *Gunfighter*
-Blue Flag — *Warrior*

Growth in Basic Training was marked by phases. A phase was a rite of passage ceremony that occurred triweekly. The titles Patriot, Gunfighter or Warrior didn't really mean as much to you at the time than the color of the flag you were graduating to. The flags symbolized growth, a calendar marker, respect and Gatorade. That's right, Gatorade! When you moved out of the red phase, you were rewarded with liberties. We could go to the shop down the street and make phone calls during our down time. We were free slaves for about an hour or two once a week, but that was our time. I don't recall the flag donning ceremony or the look on everybody's faces the first time we were honored by the changing of the flag, but I do recall what I was drinking, an icy cold Gatorade! It was the first variety of drink in weeks and it tasted like heaven. I had it by myself at the back of the shop. From the moment I took it out of the fridge door, I clutched the bottle with every muscle in my body. This drink was all mine and I was going to enjoy it, and after three long weeks, I was not disappointed as it slipped down my throat like air traveling to my lungs. I know I sound like a commercial for Gatorade, but I smiled so hard that electrolytes were dripping out my facial muscles. I was on top of a tiny world, but it was my small world if only for a second and a drink.

The thing about phases, however, is you start smelling yourself when everything starts running smoothly. You get cocky, I mean. Why wouldn't you?

You're conducting PT like a pro.

You can dismantle your weapon in less than a minute.

And you can march in step while singing a cadence.

Yep, by week six, we were the sh!# just about the time that we were gonna transition to the blue phase. And that is when it all came tumbling down. The day of our phase transition, we lined up for formation as usual with a tad bit more swagger than in days past. Standing tall with our chests pushed out, mouths dripping with grins and eyes wagging with confidence, we were ready for first formation of the day. With that much swag dripping from our pores, we may or may not have been chatting it up after coming to attention, a minor offense for a group of soldiers that had been killing it and one which, in my opinion, should have been overlooked.

Well, Drill Sergeant Bauer did not look at it as a little offense and went nuts! It went something like this: "You sorry SOBs! You think you've made it? I'm not around and this is how you act?"

He gestured to the flag with an adamant point. "That flag don't make you sh!#!" He pointed to his heart, pounding it with his finger. "This makes you a soldier! Not some damn cloth! You know what I'm gonna do since you don't know how to act?"

He stormed over to our guidon held by our platoon sergeant and yanked our white flag. Then, adding insult to injury, he balled it up and propelled it into outer space. I've never seen a cloth travel so far. He was beet-red pissed and a pissed Drill Sergeant Bauer meant one of us soldiers could be next to catapult into the air. We went from gunfighters to zeroes in a matter of a snatch. It was insane! What he yelled next is what hurt the most. He screamed, "You bunch of soup sandwiches do not deserve to be warriors! That blue flag is an honor you are never going to see."

More insanity!

Great news to receive at top of the morning and we still had to perform the rest of the day. All this occurred in front of our company and they did not feel sorry for us one bit. You could see laughter dripping from their faces with their sly smirks and gagged giggles. We were officially the laughing stocks of the company. Six weeks of training went out the window with the tossing of a single little white flag.

All this gloom and doom surrounding our platoon meant nothing to the day's tasks that we still had to complete. We had a couple of minor missions to accomplish, including Army values training and practice for drill and ceremony. However, the big one that I had no idea how we were going to find the strength to focus on was the obstacle course. After our ass chewing, we marched what was now a short 5K hike for us, but with all that was going down, we dragged our feet, carving a trench all the way to the course. When we arrived, we received a brief break, a time to gather and chat, though all anyone seemed to want to talk about from the other platoons was the stripping of our mane. One of the first people to find his way over to us was a guy no one could stand named Bradley from 1st Platoon. His drill sergeant, Burress, was a jerk and the soldiers all inherited his personality. Without so much as a hello, he strolled up to our little gathering and cockily said, "So, without a phase flag, can you graduate?"

By instinct we simultaneously grabbed Malachi, who leapt from his seated position to rip his head off. Bradley giggled, knowing he had done his job of getting under our skin, and strutted away, snickering to himself. The funny thing about adversity is that it can either crush you or it can make you stronger. Gathered in the same area and with our break almost over, we looked around at each other and knew we had two paths we could go down, the path of triumph or the path of defeat. My platoon was a scrappy bunch and different than the others. I guess that's the story of my life. I was amongst a group of outsiders who were fish out of water even when they were in the ocean.

The time for pity was over and though we knew we weren't going to get our flag back, we had to pick ourselves up from our boot straps and forge on. The obstacle course was the perfect place to do that. It was the place where platoons were pitted against each other to determine supremacy. This wasn't an all-out battle royale event or anything, but rather a challenge that sent competitors in waves to test their mettle against the other platoons. The course was pretty elaborate, as in "American Ninja Warrior" elaborate. It included: a million-foot wall, an old school tire component, a ropes course, a barbed wire crawl, a log swing, a mud pit, a spider web, a wooden ladder climb, a skinny bridge, a shuttle run home, and monkey bars. Maybe it wasn't "American Ninja Warrior," but this was 1998, so we were first. Right before we started, Drill Sergeant Bauer still couldn't stand to set eyes in our direction. Still, we gazed back in his direction, determined to earn his trust back. He yelled, "Go!"

And we were off! Wave after wave, we were let off. I wasn't a great athlete, but I could hold my own. When it was my turn to go, I knew I was doing it for God and platoon, so failure wasn't an option. Standing at the starting point, my blood galloped through my veins, drawing goose bumps and rapid heart pumps. I surveyed my competition and the reps from the second and third platoons were scrubs. One had a gigantic head that didn't look that aerodynamic and the other, well, let's just say that he was in the slow-runners club and I had inside knowledge of his performance standards. Here was the Big Kahuna. In my wave, there was Bradley, the jerk from before, and though Malachi wanted first blood, I drew the lucky chance. We locked eyes seconds into walking to the line. My bloodshot eyes screamed that I hated him and his beady eyes shouted conceit.

I heard, "Go!"

I busted off from the jump ahead of my pack, stretching my lanky legs to their fullest. *Thump!* Just like that, I was face first in the hard dirt. The crew whizzed past me on its way to the giant wall.

I picked up my pride and my body off the ground, and dashed off toward the wall. Within seconds, I caught up to the big-headed blur, but the rest had made it up and over. As previously assessed, this dude was like a bobble-head with head weights keeping him from elevating over the wall. He kept bashing his head against the wall as I took it in a couple of bounds, passing him by. One down and two to go. I was only feet behind the slow mo and yards behind Bradley when we arrived at the tire course. As expected, Slow Mo's lack of athleticism caught up to him fast.

He took every tire one by one without any hop or spring in his step, just careful precision meant for crocheting. I took a quick second to peek in his direction with bewilderment draped across my face as I zoomed by him. All I had left was the jerk face Bradley and I seemed to be pulling closer to him. Up the ropes course, under the barbed wire, onto the log swing, over the mud pit, up the wooden ladder, across the skinny bridge, and through the monkey bars, we zipped as fast as we could. With every event, I was pulling closer, but time was running out. I was running out of course and, hence, time to catch up and pass. We hit the spider web and with his first hiccup, Bradley's foot tangled and caught just long enough for me to pull even. With a real chance upon me now, Malachi screamed from the sidelines, "Take his heart, Saleem, for the dog pound!"

It was time and all that was left was the shuttle run home. Our respective platoons were going bananas! Neck to neck, we lowered ourselves down off the spider web. Both of us stumbled and tried to catch our balance. We were dead even. Huffing and puffing, I was out of breath and physically spent trying to catch up. He was no better, pale-faced and raining sweat. Deadlocked in this grudge match, I inhaled air to the deepest part of my body, oxygenating even my toes. Bound forward, I pushed ahead of this idiot Bradley. To his credit, Bradley did not just fold and flailed his arms to propel him forward. It was too late, however, as the thunderous cheers from my platoon rushed against my back like wind to a sail, thrusting me forward and a foot ahead of Bradley. Crossing the line head-first like an Olympian, my arms rose above my head in victory as Bradley sunk in defeat, not even crossing the end mark. My platoon greeted me with an array of different high fives. That was pretty much the theme of the afternoon as we demolished all of the other platoons. We did this all while wearing the stains of humiliation, but also with our heads held high. We put aside our troubles that day and acted like professionals.

As we marched back in at the end of the day, Drill Sergeant Bauer pulled us aside, threw on a smirk and then proceeded to smoke the hell out of us just for giggles. We did not cough, but inhaled his smoke and worked harder. We decided then and there that a flag was not going to define who we were for the last six weeks. Drill Sergeant Bauer called us to attention, pulled a blue flag out of his pocket and said, "Hoah!"

That was the Army term that could be a noun, verb, adverb, adjective and motivational speech, but this time it translated to, "Great job today, soldiers!" He didn't give us a speech at the end of the day like in the movies or pat us on the back. We didn't need it. We had learned our lesson. Complacency costs only a flag now, but lives later. That's what I took from it years later. At the time, I was just proud we got our flag back. I was seventeen years old with the depth of a six-year-old.

24

Fireguard

THE LIFE OF A SOLDIER ROTATES around the details. Not details describing individual features or facts, but details that in the Army world describes various job assignments. As a new recruit, we were not immune to this word known as *details* and if anything, Basic Training was the perfect time to indoctrinate us into this world.

In fact, *fireguard* was our first opportunity to get our feet wet for our future life as the Army's finest. Fireguard is also one of the most boring details in the history of details. You sit down on a chair in the middle of a hall without a book, phone or computer and wait for a fire to happen or not happen. I have a jar filled with imaginary hours I have wasted in my life that I will never get back and a majority of them were accumulated at fireguard.

The fact that fireguard mainly takes place around the hours of sleep time, and I highly value my sleep, made it not an ideal job for me. Miraculously, we were about six- and-a-half weeks in before I was assigned to the guard for the first time, and drew the late shift. I hopped up on my bunk the night before, ready for the challenge.

I was equipped with all my supplies in tow:

-Torch
-Orange reflector vest
-Positive attitude

I tucked them underneath my pillow and closed my eyes, at peace with myself for being prepared. Hours later, the lights were on and I had a group of angry roommates staring daggers in my direction. Tovis, the soft-spoken, tough-but-gentle Californian Samoan that I roomed with, had a look of fury in his eyes. His eyes got redder and twitched as he described to me in detail the many efforts he went through to try and wake me up.

"First I was gentle with you, promise, but then the angrier I got that you were playing dead, I shook more and more. But you didn't wake up, bro, and guess who pulled a double shift at two in the morning. The F.U. of times to go to sleep. Me! You're going to pay for this!"

I had not seen this side of him to this point. Overnight, I had destroyed his positive energy and created a vengeful asshole. I had committed the number-one offense of soldier brotherhood: Don't leave a fellow soldier twisting in the wind. We had a long day ahead of us and my brother Tovis had pulled a double shift because of me. I had my first blue falcon moment of my life and it sucked. Now a pariah in the room, I found it hard to find anyone that would interact with me all day. Getting the cold shoulder sucks, but getting the cold shoulder in Basic is like the scarlet letter with an S standing for sucks in this instance.

When we arrived back to the barracks that night, I sauntered into the room just wanting to find the embrace of my bed. Circled around my bunk, however, were the guys. This was a Basic Training intervention of sorts. I stuttered over my words, "Tovis, I am really sorry and will do anything to make it up to you."

Tovis looked at the guys and then back at me, and calmly stated, "You'll pull Rosen's fireguard tonight."

I responded, "Sure, no problem!"

But he wasn't done. Tovis replied in his calm voice, "You also have to sneak downstairs and bring us back an item off of the sergeant on duty's desk."

My mind rattled and spun, screaming, "NO!"

My mouth said with a shaky voice, "Yeah, sure, no problem," against all reason.

That night I woke up for my duty pretty easily at 0100 hours and forty-two seconds, maybe because I never went to sleep. Nope, I wasn't taking any risks. I sat down on the duty chair under the red, illuminated exit sign, mustering up the courage to do my duty, for room and country. As the clock on the wall ticked and ticked, time flew by with my task hanging over my head. Even though I had this additional burden, I tried to take in my first fireguard experience. I had about an hour to do so, and this was the first time I had all to myself, in a long while, to reflect on my Basic experience. I wondered what my parents would say to me now that I made it this far and didn't die. Sure, the bar was set really low, but the fact remains that I had survived to this point. I also couldn't help think what Margarita was up to? She was going through her own Basic experience. She had written me a couple of letters, but there is only so much the page can hold.

I could never explain to people who knew me that I had changed so much and still remained the same. Sitting in that chair, I was giving myself a full psychological evaluation for free. *Who needs a therapist?* I could have used a psychic, however, because who was winning the home run race between Sammy and Mark was still a burning question on my mind that none of the Drills felt obligated to keep us updated on. *Baseball history, folks, from 1998!* Before I knew it, the time had flown by and I only had ten minutes left to gain redemption. It was now or never.

I stared down that scary, dark stairwell downstairs. If this were a horror film, everybody would be screaming for me not to go. *Black guy, you'll die!* But like in the movies, the naive black guy with the trembling knees heads in *that* direction. As I reached the base of the stairwell, I could hear faint baseball game sounds. I had reached the lion's den. I peeked around the corner and saw Drill Sergeant Graham reclined back in a chair. He was the same drill sergeant, ironically, who tried to kill us that fateful day in the slow group run. His slightly rotund stomach pulsated with laughter as he watched the Cardinals play. *Damn it.* It was Mark McGwire on

TV. I could just stay here, watch the game and find out the home run update. But no, I had a mission that I needed to stay on and sneaking in was now ruled out. So plan B it was. I strolled into the room and fell into parade rest to the displeasure of Drill Sergeant Graham. I didn't say it was a good plan. He snapped at me, "What the hell are you doing recruit?"

I stuttered, "Ah, I need to, I mean, I want a pen, please, for my fireguard log."

He snarled, rolled his eyes and turned around, reaching back to search for a pen. This was my opportunity. I scanned the desk, looking for something that would get me out of the dog house. Eureka! There was a bowl of nondescript hard candies. Just before he turned back around, I swiped a few and stuffed them in my pocket. Drill Sergeant Graham handed me the pen and then, as if he knew what I had done, he studied the top of his desk. He looked me up and down with suspicious eyes. I shot him a nervous smile and pointed to his TV screen. I said, "So did Slammin' Sammy or Mark McGwire get the record yet?"

He reclined back in his chair and frowned, replying, "Not yet, recruit, but soon."

I was home free, but a pocketful of candy just didn't feel right or worth redemption. I needed something bigger. So with a little more confidence, I said, "I am so sorry, Drill Sergeant, I really need paper too. The book is full."

He frowned and squinted his eyes at me with distrust and replied, "I don't know what you recruits write down to fill up these books, but I know fireguard isn't that exciting."

He turned around once again in his swivel chair. Knowing that I didn't have long, I reached for an item, any item, on the desk. But as fast as he swiveled around to look, he swiveled right back and I had to retract my hands just as fast. He came back around as I nonchalantly rubbed my sweaty hands behind me in parade rest like everything was normal. "So, say again, you are telling me that whole notebook is full?"

He was asking too many questions now, but I couldn't show weakness, so I retorted, "It is almost the seventh week, Drill Sergeant, and this is the first change in notebooks, Drill Sergeant." He could look back and nod his head with an answer that tight!

He turned his chair back around and without hesitation, I snatched the first item I saw and stuffed it into my cargo pocket. He rotated back around and handed me the book. Automatically, I pulled it from his hand but he held tight, yanking me back. He then drew me in by the book and intensely asked, "Are you a Cardinals fan, soldier?"

Nervous, because I was a Mets fan and didn't want to lie, but knowing I had to be calm because this was a question testing my trust, I replied, "Since the days of Ozzie Smith!"

A grin slowly grew across his face.

"I knew it. You have that honest look to you. Now get back upstairs, soldier, and watch out for fires."

I scurried back upstairs before he changed his mind.

At the top of the stairwell, I stopped, pumped my fists a couple times, and felt like I was alive and brave.

The next morning as "God Bless the USA" played over the loudspeakers and the lights were popped on by the fireguard, all the guys looked over in my direction. Their eyes asked the same question, "Did you get it?"

I pulled out the assortment of hard candy from underneath my pillow and held it in the air like a lion's head hunted from the wild. The jaws in the room dropped as if it were a lion's head. I hopped down off my bunk and presented the candy to Tovis. He shot me a head nod and with a handshake, we were all good. Before he pulled away, I drew him back in and with my other hand, I handed him the other bounty. It was a customized pen engraved with "Be all you can be" on top of it. A smile popped on his face and he tugged me back in to squeeze the life out of me with an old-school Samoan bear hug. We were really all good now. In fact, the whole room was good with me as everyone came over and hit me with fives. We all let people down sometimes, but it is what we are willing to do to show them our loyalty that counts.

25

The Grenade

I N THE MOVIES, USING A GRENADE SEEMS SIMPLE. You see a bad guy, take out the pin, and toss it in the right direction. In reality, even this seemingly simple act requires training.

As a platoon, you go to the grenade yard and train on the proper techniques of throwing, all without tossing a single grenade. The drill sergeants train you to throw a grenade like a football and hours later, you are tested without ever throwing a live one. So when the drill sergeant thought I did not throw the grenade to the right degree of technique, I failed without ever throwing a single grenade. I was utterly humiliated.

The ex-high school football player could not throw a make-believe football. I was sent to the bolo pool and rescheduled to throw the grenades with the dud group. Upon my return home, I had to endure hearing my fellow recruits talk about their grenade tosses, and mixed into those stories were chunks of ridicule for just one individual, me. When you fail at something in Basic , they work hard on getting you right back on the horse. So they did just that, sending me right back out to the grenade grounds the very next day.

The next morning, I joined a special formation filled with a collection of reject soldiers from our battalion. Let's just say if we were creating an Army super-soldier calendar, none of them would be on it. I felt like I was better than the lot and did not belong with them. One girl, however, did stick out to me. She was different. Her caramel complexion shimmered in the sun, her smile captivated the souls of her misfit group, and an energy vibrated from her body like the bass of an amp. She was gorgeous and the only bright point of waking up that morning. The whole march over to the grenade grounds, I couldn't help but stare over in her direction. I loved everything about her, from the way she strutted with her Yorkshire-size legs to her Kool-Aid grin reaching from cheek to cheek, and right down to the way she wore her Basic , no-frills haircut. She was perfect without trying, but I knew she was from another company and it would never work. This was a fantasy and I had to get focused really quick or I would fail again.

When we arrived at the grenade grounds, I segregated myself from the group and started practicing throwing an imaginary football. There was a determination in my throws as my imaginary footballs went farther and farther, my velocity increasing with every throw. I was going to be Dan Marino for the day and there would be no stopping me. The others weren't training at all, but playing tag and tumbling in the grass like kindergartners, so I felt better about myself because I was dedicated. They did, however, seem to be having more fun than me, laughing and smiling. I stuck to my guns and continued to progress through my fundamentals but was surely jealous of how loose they were. The Drills did not waste time getting us right into action. We all zipped through the throwing test with ease, almost as if this were a sham test. I mean, I didn't throw any differently than last time. Also, the pimply kid next to me, with the muscles of a limp noodle and weighing all of twenty pounds, threw the imaginary grenade like he was throwing an anvil. No, it seemed like we were being made an example of to keep the rest of the soldiers in our companies from getting complacent. I knew I didn't really fail the first time. They failed me.

As we moved to the live grenade part of the day, I was pretty down that my pride was sacrificed to make a point. I couldn't help think while the drill sergeant gave us the safety briefing, *What is the point? They probably pull and throw the grenade for you.*

The first sap to go into the bunker with the drill sergeant had knees shaking the whole way through the door. I was no longer worried, however, because this was all a sham anyway and he was a lock to pass. No, I'd made up my mind and I might as well hang out with the loose group because at least they were having fun. I eased on over to the group of misfits that I had shunned earlier and sat like I had been cool with them all along.

Funny thing about shunning though; as I was segregating myself from them, they were doing the same thing to me. One soldier sitting there in the inner circle, Riley, an Italian kid from Alpha 110 company, said, "Look who decided to join us. Super soldier."

Everyone snickered right away. I had become an inside joke in such a short period of time. My body shrank and my cheeks began to harden with embarrassment. I started to push myself up to walk away and then I relaxed my arms, smiled and said, "You're right, I was taking this way too seriously, but did you see how far I can throw an imaginary football now?"

A smile slowly grew across Riley's face and then he burst into a laugh that infected the group within milliseconds. Even my imaginary wife for the day slumped back into her arms, blushing, and grinned. Riley replied, "I was just busting your balls. We get it, you can't afford to fail. The thing is, none of us are going to fail. This is just a sham. We all got this in the bag."

I calmly retorted, "I know now."

Riley went on to introduce the rest of the group, but I was caught in a dream ending with the name Thomas. I had surmised from some nifty sleuth detective work — I looked at her name tag her name was Thomas. Yep, I figured if I stared at her long enough, it would be as if we were talking. She whispered sweet nothings in my direction, *I am so happy I failed my first grenade challenge so that I could be here with your amazing face. If we had more time and a dark room, I would…*

All of a sudden, *Boom!*

The blast bumped me out of my imaginary first date with Thomas and two seconds later, that same kid who went in first was tossed out of the bunker. He probably slid on his Kevlar for twenty feet before coming to a rest. The drill stomped out of the doorway mad as dog sh!#, yelling profanities. He turned to us and said in a most evil voice, "If you throw the Goddamn grenade, you better make sure you clear the wall. Because if I have another incident like this ate- up-sorry-excuse-for-a-soldier just did, I'll slam you so hard that you will never be right enough to finish Basic . He is a no go!"

We stood there shocked with our jaws out and all I could think was, This has just become real. Riley and the rest of the crew picked up the quickest grenade-throwing stance I had ever seen. Thomas, as cool as the other side of the pillow, sat there with a calm face. I marveled at her cool demeanor, which calmed me down. It seemed nothing rattled her and I had to project the same because, after all, we were husband and wife for the day. *A team!*

Then I heard the words, "You're next, Saleem!"

I nearly wet the bed. I turned to the drill sergeant and he signaled for me to come now. I tried to maintain my cool and walk over to him calmly, but I scurried over there with a mixture of speed walk and sprint. I got halfway to the bunker entrance and just froze a la Cameron from *Ferris Bueller's Day Off* when his car drives out of the garage and into the ditch. I stood there for a second and questioned whether I would become that kid who didn't get it over the wall. I felt a soothing breath on my cheek and heard the sweetest voice whisper in my ear, "You can do it, Saleem. Go for it."

I smiled and angled back towards her direction, but in that very instant, I heard, "Saleem!

Get your ass down here!"

I snapped out of my trance and hurried over to the bunker door, fumbling and tumbling over the grass with anxiety. I slid on my flak jacket and took one last glance at Thomas, thinking it could be my last sight of her. She was the one and only one not in stitches ridiculing me.

Inside the bunker, it looked like a battlefield with dummy targets fixed everywhere. The drill sergeant ushered me over behind the infamous "wall of protection." At first, I was disappointed in the wall that the kid couldn't throw the grenade over. It was only five-by-five feet! An Oompa Loompa with amputated legs could surely clear the structure. That was what I thought until I got behind it and the Drill handed me the live grenade. He looked at me and gritted out twelve precise words: "You have ten seconds once you've pulled the pin to throw it."

The drill must have enchanted magical words because as soon as he finished saying them, I pulled the pin and we were live. When people say I move in slow motion when accomplishing a task, I always grin. Whatever. I can honestly say that time slowed to a crawl and I became hyper-focused on my training. I stood, pulled the pin, gave my best Usain Bolt victory pose, and tossed the grenade like a football. I ducked behind the wall and *Boom!* I wish any of my stories ended with the drill sergeant giving me a high-five, but that is never the case. I walked out the door and he simply said, "Next!"

I don't know how the rest of the guys in the room felt after tossing one, but I know that I felt vindicated. Our accompanying drill lined us up. Instead of us all going back together, we split up into different companies. I looked over for one last glance at Thomas and waved. Her company was immediately called to attention and marched away, but while the drill sergeant was not looking, she turned around and quickly flashed me a wave. My hard knock's lesson for the day was simple. You only fail when you give up. There was also one more lesson—women like men who make things go Boom!

26

Home Run Race

SOME PEOPLE'S VICES ARE SMOKING, drinking, or overeating. Well, mine was sports. Sports were the only thing that made sense to me as a kid. Sports were also one of the only ways that my father and I could have sensible communication. So, in the summer of '98 when I was stuck in Ft. Leonard Wood, MO, I was at the total mercy of the drill sergeants for any sports information.

I was going through serious withdrawal from ESPN and this was the summer of all summers for sports. Mark McGwire and slamming Sammy Sosa were going head to head for the home run record, and I was missing it. So every morning like clockwork, I'd wake up and find the courage to approach a drill sergeant and ask him about the race. I'd like to say that all of the interactions were positive, or that actually I'd like to say that any of them were positive. No, every morning on cue, they'd promptly scream at me or worse, dropping me into the front lean and rest position. They did not understand that the next time I spoke with my dad, I wanted to go into the conversation informed. We had limited time for a phone call, so I didn't want to waste it on backstory.

As the summer dragged on and our phases increased, we were allowed to make phone calls home on Sunday. If we were lucky, we got two in a week. The phone calls gave us only enough time to let our families know we were alive, similar to a kidnapper's proof-of-life call. I was relegated to getting sports updates solely from my dad in five-minute recaps. It was about half the time of our conversations but enough time to really dig into the subject. My dad enjoyed giving me these updates and I enjoyed hearing his voice. The only sport going on that summer was baseball, and by baseball I mean the Slammin' Sammy and Mark McGwire home run race.

They were hitting home runs in bunches of ten at a time, it seemed like. This was the favorite part of my conversations but also the saddest. I was missing out on a piece of sports history, hearing it a week later. Close to the end of Basic Training, I had given up on asking my morning question. I was like the rest of the herd and walked down to formation in the morning, waiting for the instruction of the day. Roger Maris's record of sixty-one home runs had fallen already, but the home run race was still going on and I was gonna be the last person to know if it was Mark or Sammy. It was time for me to focus my energy on soldiering and leave the sports world in the past.

On the Friday of our seventh week, we were getting our phone call home earlier in the week than usual for some reason. It had something to do with training and was important. All I knew was that I didn't really care as much this time. I just wanted to do my time and leave that world behind. I knew if my father answered, he'd suck me right in. I picked up the receiver on the pay phone and waited as it rang. My dad, as expected, picked up the phone that day and greeted me with, "*Assalamualaikum*."

I replied with sorrow in my voice, "*Walaikum salam*."

My father could sense something was wrong and said, "Sammy hit another home run, and that puts him tied with Mark at sixty-five."

My heart wasn't in it though and I replied, "That's nice. How are Mom, Amir and Zayd?" I could hear the confusion in his voice as he said, "They're fine, but is everything okay, buddy?"

I started to lie, as all people do when something is wrong, but before I could get the words out, I stopped and said, "Yes, there is something wrong. Why do we always have to talk sports? Why can't we just talk about what's going on in our lives?"

Stunned, my dad went silent. I don't think he expected this straightforwardness from me.

But before he could reply, Drill Sergeant Bauer screamed, "Time's up!"

Time's up really meant time's up when Drill Sergeant Bauer said it, and I had to leave my dad hanging.

"Talk later, Dad. I gotta run," and then I hung up. I felt

bad, but If I had learned anything those few weeks, it was that a man says what's on his mind. At least that's what my drill sergeants always did, and they weren't afraid of anything.

A couple of days went by after that and the Monday of our eighth week was here. The tunnel was getting brighter and, for the first time, it didn't seem like a train was coming through it, but that there were shimmers of light from the other side. As we were standing in formation, ready for the training of the day, our head drill, Buchanan, came out as usual and called us to attention. He screamed, "Mark McGwire has just won the home run race for everyone who has been asking."

A loud roar echoed across the Missouri blue sky. I glanced around and the whole of Delta 110 was cheering and hooting. I realized at that moment, I was far from the only one asking, and that the home run race was far more than just about sports. That race was a message of hope to all of us sports fans trying to make it through Basic Training. It was a loud scream saying, "You can do this!" I know it was cheesy, but it was true. My father knew that and, though he could have spoken about all sorts of family thrills and dramas, he chose to try and fill me with hope during this period, and in return, I filled him with grief. He had a week to feel like sh!# and that was on me, and I had no idea how to make it right.

At the end of the day, we were dismissed from final formation. Before I could run upstairs, Drill Sergeant Graham, my old friend from the fireguard heist, stopped me. I stood firm, knowing that if he waited two weeks to accuse me, now he had no evidence. He approached and I snapped into parade rest. He said, "At ease, soldier. From one Cardinal fan to another, how great is it Mark beating old Sammy in the long ball race?"

Again, not a Cardinals fan, but I had committed to my alter ego and I had to see it through. "It's fantastic! I can't wait to talk to my father about this on Sunday."

He smiled and replied, "I know it's great. That's all, soldier. You're almost there. Get upstairs." I stood my ground and looked him in the eyes. He awkwardly looked back at me and said, "That was all, soldier. Get out of here."

Steadfast in my resolve, I stood there and stared into his eyes and said, "Drill Sergeant, I had a huge fight with my father about not wanting to hear about the race on our last phone call, but it was because I was angry at something else and took it out on him. Please let me make it right and call him for a few minutes right now."

He studied me up and down as if to say in his head, *The balls on this one.*

I figured let me lay it all out on the line. What did I have to lose? *My ass, that's what!* He smoked the hell out of me for ten minutes, saying over and over again, "What, are we drinking buddies now?"

A couple of drill sergeants, remnants of the formation, laughed at me before going inside. I yelled in my head, *Don't go.* They were the only witnesses to this ongoing murder attempt, and now we were alone. He shouted, "To your feet, soldier!"

I strained to stand. He surveyed the area from left to

right. One last peek before finishing me off. He gazed into my eyes and said, "Had to make it look good. You have five minutes. Now go before my constituents come back. Can't have them think I play favorites. Go, Cardinals!"

I whispered, "Thank you, Drill Sergeant Graham!"

I dashed over to the pay phone, fumbled the receiver before recovering and dialed the number. My father picked up the phone again and before he could get a word out edgewise, I said, "What do you think about Mark winning the race?"

He paused for a second, laughed and went on with the theme of the conversation. This time I had a crazy story of how I stole something off this drill sergeant's desk, then he thought I was a Cardinals fan, and that led him to trying to kill me before he allowed me to make this phone call. We went a little deeper than just sports this time and for me, it was hands-down one of the best days at Basic Training.

27

Fraternization

THERE IS A SAYING I HEARD THROUGHOUT my military career, "If it ain't raining, it ain't training."

Therefore, with a week and a half left in Basic , I was stunned when a torrential downpour drove our early morning PT gallop under the field house. I was still a road guard and sat in the front of the formation with the other road guards as we waited for the rains to subside. At the rate the buckets of water were dumping down on Earth, that didn't look like anytime soon.

Great minds think alike and we weren't the only ones with the idea of staying dry. Bravo Company dashed under the field house minutes after us. They were soggy, they were tired and they were the keepers of the girl of my dreams!

There was Thomas, the girl from the grenade range! It didn't take long for her to see me either as our eyes locked. She slowed to a crawl in my eyes as she strutted to her sitting place right in front of me, and only fifteen feet away. She wore the yellow reflector belt across the gray winter uniform with black lettering that read "Army" on top. It was the same as the rest of us, but it looked exquisite on her. *It was fate!* What were the chances that I would see the same girl from a different company twice in the span of a week? *Terrible really, that's what!*

The universe was talking to me and I needed to take action. So I made the first move and stalked her with my eyes until she broke off conversation with her friend and gave me her undivided attention. Then I smiled. She blushed and flashed me a full smile, not knowing what to do to reciprocate, but her smile was all I needed. We made eyes at each other while the raindrops hit the galvanized roofing. Trading smile for smile, we almost forgot where we were, or simply didn't care. All I can say is that I'm happy I didn't impregnate her with my ogling. She moved her mouth, asking, "What was your name?"

Honestly, I was a little hurt at first because I knew her name, but I was too overcome with joy to let petty hurt get in the way and mouthed back, "Saleem."

She shook her head and laughed. Then mouthed, "Your first."

Phew, she knew my name. Feelings unhurt. I replied, "Khalid. And yours?"

She mouthed back, "Angel." *Okay, not really. It was Denise, but in some galaxy it probably means angel. Why not here?*

The rain was beginning to let up and our love story was

ending. We were lost for words and content with our playful grins for however longer this fairy tale would last. The pitter-patter on the roof ceased and we both sank into the dirt in despair. Mirroring each other's sadness, I watched her lift her body up off the ground. She wiped a tear from her eye, not because she loved me or anything crazy like that, but because it's hard to find that snap connection with people in the real world and doubly hard within Basic Training. Her company wasted no time as they formed up, and I had to watch her once again leave my life. My company was also ready to hop up and go, so I gathered with the other road guards. Set to run off and get on with my life, I was summoned along with three others by four of our drill sergeants. The first thing we were asked was, "Which one of you were making eyes at that pretty little private in the other company?"

First rule you learn as a kid is make them tell you how much information they actually have on you. The drills looked around at the four of us shaking our heads in denial and I thought I was safe; just keep on shaking my head and playing dumb. That is when they pulled out the big guns and a drill said, "Okay, if none of you are going to tell the truth, I guess we have to issue Article 15s to all of you and chapter each and every one of you out."

An Article 15 was a clerical punishment by the Army that could strip you of rank and money, and in Basic Training that meant possible discharge or being recycled. *Not good! I had come too far and was not starting over!* I cracked immediately. *Don't ever rob a bank with me. I'm not that guy!* I screamed, "It was me! I did it!"

In a snap, the Drills sent the other three away and I was the last man standing. By the eighth week, I thought I heard all the insults, but they still had some tricks up their sleeves and got creative with their harsh remarks. They surrounded me and didn't scream but showered me with sadistic whispers. First, Drill Sergeant Boon said, "So you think she loves you, huh? With your small ears and rough hands."

Then Drill Sergeant Spivey jumped in, "No, no, Drill, he's in love. Probably don't have pube hair, but he knows what love is."

There's nothing like a female's insults. Drill Sergeant Coleman chimed in, "You think he even knows what to do with his thing-thing?"

Drill Sergeant Chow just couldn't resist adding his two cents and finished me off. "He couldn't know how to use his willy. He's a virgin from the Virgin Islands."

Everyone burst into laughter and thought that last statement was the absolute funniest. The first sergeant, who happened to be in the neighborhood then, jogged over, soaked as a wet dog, and asked, "What's this sorry sack of dog sh!# doing here?"

The other drills filled him in on what I thought was a minor offense. Nothing of the sort. First Sergeant Snur screwed his face up in every direction as they retold what happened. It went from innocent flirting to a lewd, perverted act of a deviant. He signaled for Head Drill Sergeant Buchanan to come over. Then Snur uttered the words that nearly made me sh!# my pants, "Kick him out!"

Drill Sergeant Buchanan was even taken aback as well as the other drill sergeants, who backed up a bit when he released those words. Drill Sergeant Buchanan wanted to make sure he heard him right. "So you want me to kick him out?" Without hesitation, Snur repeated, "Yeah, kick him out, recycle him. I just don't want him in my unit." He began strolling away like he was just releasing air, but he turned around for one last jab: "Yeah, recycle him. That's a worse death. Maybe that son of a bitch will learn to keep his eyes to himself."

I could deal with getting kicked out. It would suck, but the moment he said recycle, my feet grew roots as I couldn't move. I got back to the barracks, but my legs, when they eventually started working, were in autopilot.

Back at the barracks, the Drills had me wait in the lobby of their office area. I had only been in there a couple of times but not for any long period. The walls were littered with awards, guidons and pictures of past drill sergeants. There was a lot of history there and now I was a part of it, sitting in the seat of shame. My friends walked past me, shooting looks of support and thumbs-up gestures. They believed this was probably the last they would see of me. I sat out there for what seemed an eternity but really was an hour. That's when the head drill sergeant came out, holding a stack of documents in a folder labeled "Saleem." I presumed that those were my chapter paperwork. This just went from surreal to *real*. Drill Sergeant Buchanan asked, "Saleem, what were you thinking?"

I lowered my head and opened my mouth to say

something, and then he exploded into a diatribe. "I know what you were thinking. Fu@$ you, Drill Sergeant Buchanan! Because guess who now has to type up paperwork on your stupid behind. You were so damn close, Private Saleem, and you chose to throw it away over a skirt."

I was so messed up in the head at this point, I actually thought Thomas and I had intercourse. It was just smiling, people, not a gesture of porn! He continued on reading me the riot act and picked up the phone. "Saleem, you stupid, stupid boy. Do you want to call your parents and explain to them you failed?"

I did not cry on the outside, but inside I was and disseminating a little pee into my brown undies in tiny increments. I couldn't tell them that I was a failure like they thought. I couldn't tell them that I didn't survive Basic like everyone had predicted. I couldn't make that phone call.

As Drill Sergeant Buchanan sat there with the receiver in his hand, my eye wells swelled with tears, but before one could drop, I sucked them back up. I might have been getting kicked out, but I wasn't going to cry because I did not regret anything. I'd smile at Thomas a thousand more times over. I had to take my punishment like a man. I straightened up, raised my chest and looked in his direction, ready for my punishment. The moment I wasn't afraid anymore, something changed in him and he analyzed my posture. He slowly hung up the phone. Drill Sergeant Buchanan then finished up with this: "Soldier, you are almost done and it would cost more money to kick you out than actually let you finish, so straighten up your act. You can start by volunteering to give blood today."

This time I was the one jerking my head back in disbelief. I let out a sigh of relief and said, "Yes, Drill Sergeant!"

I don't know if the whole thing was B.S. or he really was on the verge of kicking me out, but I would gladly give a little blood for my salvation. He told me to go and report to a formation that would shortly leave to go to the clinic. I had never been so relieved in my life. I had defied death and now only had to deal with my fear of needles. It sounded like a fair tradeoff to me.

Outside the clinic doors, my mind wandered while we waited. I could not stop thinking of the angel I had seen twice in the most peculiar of circumstances. This had to mean something, right? Was it the biggest of life's teases, mere coincidence?

Once I was checked into my Manila- colored stall and my blood was cleared, I waited and smiled, thinking that, meaning or no meaning, it gave me a memory. As the memory became permanent in my brain, I closed my eyes, but before I could get comfortable, the curtains pulled back. With God as my witness, it was Denise Thomas standing before me. Yeah, this kind of magic only happens in movies and I was living it. Thomas, who was on detail as a volunteer, took my blood. We stood there smiling and blushing like silly kids. It took about five minutes before we said a word to each other and by that time, she had taken my blood. We laughed at her amazing precision and the fact that she hadn't stabbed me with the needle while in autopilot mode.

Leery of being overheard, Thomas led me outside to a section of the clinic that was unsupervised. In most romance novels, this is where the story might get hot and steamy, all the raw animal attraction between us making it hard to keep our hands off each other. But sensible heads prevailed and in this tale, we simply talked and talked. It was good to just enjoy the connection we shared. We probably spoke for two hours about everything the Lord made silly on this planet. This chance meeting was as improbable and unpredictable as a rainbow in the desert. This was my rainbow and no one else's, and that felt good.

We exchanged contact information that day and even kept in contact with each other for a year after Basic . My memory of the three chance meetings with a beautiful girl named Denise Thomas was the epitome of a summer fling. I guess the lesson I learned was that chance meetings and fate are interpretations best left to be reflected on in later years, and intended to be lived exclusively in that moment.

.

28

Pushups, Sit-ups, and Run

THEN THERE WAS A LITTLE THING CALLED THE PT test that was probably going to get me recycled. The PT test consisted of three parts: the push-up, sit-ups, and run. You must meet the criteria in all those events if you didn't want to get recycled. The criterion for each was as follows:

Push-ups
100 pts = 82 completed
90 pts = 72
80 pts = 62
70 pts = 52

Sit-ups
100 pts = 92 completed
90 pts = 82

80 pts = 72
70 pts = 62

Two-mile run
100 pts = 11:54
90 pts = 12:54
80 pts = 13:54
70 pts = 14:54

To pass Basic , we just needed to clear sixty points for each event and that was the realm I was going to live in. I failed the first PT test miserably, scoring lows in all events, but I think I set records with how slow my two-mile run was. I was really worried about passing this one, but if anything was going to get me, it would be the push-up. I was getting stronger in every other section through osmosis brought on by physical abuse, but for some reason I just wasn't good at push-ups, and my muscles weren't getting any stronger despite how many we did a day.

With a couple of days till the last PT test, I decided to get my butt into gear and train. I work best under pressure. I enlisted the help of my friend Collins who was outside my platoon. I learned from the best. My core buddies had outside platoon friends. Malachi had Brownlow, a like-minded cadet who just wanted stuff done the correct way; Thompson had LeBlanc, an equally hilarious guy who ran like the wind; and I had Collins, a similar fish-out-of-water recruit who was on the verge of being kicked out at anytime. Yeah, we found our perfect doppelgangers. Collins was a tall African-American male with a Southern drawl so strong that it would make you think he was putting on a television accent. He and I both had our weaknesses. I did push- ups like I had no arms and Collins was as slow as a one-legged mule. The good news was we only had two days to get it right, but the bad news was we were the blind leading the blind.

Collins and I decided we would meet for our training during crack-of-dawn PT and after hours in my bay room. The first day of training, I instructed Collins to sneak into my running group. Once we had separated into running groups, he arrived. He stood there wide-eyed and sweaty, and we hadn't even gone anywhere. I patted his shoulders down to calm his nerves, but all I did was drench my hands in his sweat. Drill Sergeant Spivey, the leader of the speedster group, commanded, "Go!"

The group took off, but Collins froze, causing the road guards to collide into him. He wasn't making any friends in this group, but at least he was fast at doing it. I dragged him along and acted as his coach as we moseyed, not ran, but moseyed down the street. He waddled from side to side, huffing and puffing, wheezing and taking periodic rest breaks, bent over and clutching his knees like the last branch on a cliff that he was hanging on for dear life. The road guards were even more incensed by the fact that they were pretty much walking by this point. I said to Collins, "One leg after the other! That's all you have to do."

Those were my words of motivation for my battle buddy. Cliché after cliché was the mantra that I now lived by after joining Basic Training. All my words of fire seemed to be working as he made it the whole way home, running about four miles, double the required run time. I carried his limp body up the stairs. He murmured the whole way up the stairs, like a drunk swearing off alcohol forever. He was never going to win marathons, but he, by all intents and purposes, would be able to pass the two-mile run.

My session began after hours in my bay room. Collins met me over there and the grin on his face told me he was in for a bit of revenge after that run earlier. I was right, he didn't even greet me with a hello, but demanded, "Drop into the push-up position, Saleem!"

His deep commanding voice scared me and I dropped into the front lean and rest position. He was in full role-playing mode and continued his routine with, "Soldier, you have to keep the back straight and the push-up only counts if you break the plain at a 45-degree angle."

I replied, "I know. I just can't. I…"

Not letting me finish my sentence, he snapped at me, "Soldier, ain't nobody tell you to talk! That's ten push-ups."

Luckily, no one else was around and could see the lunatic that he had become. For thirty minutes straight, he put me through the ringer. My arms didn't feel like they were getting stronger, just more like jello. He looked at his watch and suddenly snapped out of his crazy, possessed, drill sergeant role, saying, "Hey, Saleem, good session. I really think you made some strides today." Laid out sprawled on the floor, I strained my head up and I glared up at him. I gave him a glare to let him know I was going to hunt him down and kill him. He smiled and bopped out of the room. I guess it didn't work. We repeated the process the next day and prayed that the extensive cramming would work.

The morning of the final PT test came and I felt like throwing up. The jitters reverberated through my stomach and into my face, creating a look of worry that is hard to swipe off with just believing. The drill sergeants took us to an open field where they positioned themselves in a straight line clear across the plain. There were ten lines and every platoon aligned with its drill sergeant. The first event was the push-up, and I spotted Collins from across the field. Where I was twitching with nerves, he was bouncing with jubilation. This was his event! He hailed me with a wave and I threw one back half-heartedly. It was time to begin. The drill sergeants had us face the opposite direction from the people performing the push-ups. This made the line move like lunch time at the DMV. The line eventually got to me and Drill Sergeant Mitchell was my grader. A scowl of disappointment was plastered on her face as if I were the hundredth person in line to piss in her drink. I would surely be in trouble if I wasn't perfect in my execution. I assumed the front lean and rest position. I had an internal checklist that I kept running through in my head: flatten my back, keep arm straight, break the plain to a forty-five-degree angle, and straighten arms back out. There was no room for error. I needed thirty-two to pass and that was what I was shooting for.

When Drill Sergeant Mitchell opened her mouth to say go, I snapped like a traumatic flashback. Collins screaming at me flooded my mind and I began pumping them out, machine- gun style. I was at twenty-five before I knew it, eclipsing my mark of twenty that I previously set on my diagnostic test. He was just so angry in my head, saying things like, "Saleem, here you go into muscle failure. I am going to eat your future children for dinner." Or, "I am going to beat you like a dish rag if you don't keep pushing, soldier!"

The greatest hits of the meanest things anyone had ever said to me played in my head non-stop, and before I knew it, my arms gave out on me as Drill Sergeant Mitchell said, "Good work, Saleem. You scored thirty-seven. Next!"

I did it! Granted this was the first event in the test, but I had conquered my demon. Now I had to make sure Collins vanquished his.

After breezing through the sit-ups portion, it was time to take on the two-mile run. I didn't feel like this event was in the bag for me, but I knew I had improved significantly through shared torture over the past eight weeks. I was going to be fine, but my battle buddy was shaking like a tree in a hurricane next to me. I took him by the shoulders, as all of the recruits were lined up on a road, ready to run. I stared straight into his eyes and said, "Dude, look here. I just completed the hardest portion of my Basic Training and that was largely because of your maniacal fiery voice in my head. Now you need to channel that voice, and let's do this!"

Collins eked out a smile and replied in his slow Southern drawl, "Saleem, I'm about to kick this run's ass!"

Just like that, he was focused. Drill Sergeant Graham, who was standing on the side of the road, yelled, "Go!" A

PART II PROGRESSION REQUIREMENTS (RED PHASE)

GO	NO GO		GO	NO GO		GO	NO GO	
✓		RIFLE BAYONET TRAINING			HAND TO HAND COMBAT TRAINING	✓		PASS PHASE 1 TEST
		PUGIL FIGHTING TRAINING	✓		FOOTMARCH 3K			HOURS MISSED TRAINING

PART III COMPLETED TRAINING (RED PHASE) ALL MISSED TRAINING MUST BE MADE UP WITHIN 7 DAYS OF ADVANCEMENT TO THE NEXT PHASE

							RFT
AD	FA1	MJ2	CM	DC3	BRM1	RB1	NSO
APTB	FA2	MR1	CO	DC4	HZ/UXO	RB2	EPTS
CD	GD1	MR2	DAPFT	DC5	PT1	RB3	ELS
CHO	GD2	NBC1	EA	DC6	PT2	RB4	OTHER
CL	SA	NBC2	EO	ID1	PT3	RB5	
HH1	SC	AFTB	DC1	IN1	HT	PHH	
HH2	TH	LL	DC2	MC	SELF	AIDS	

PART IV PHYSICAL FITNESS Soldier displays effort to improve fitness level

DIAGNOSTIC PT TEST (Standard: 50 points per event) PHASE 1 PT TEST (Standard: 50 points per event)

Event	Raw Score	Score		Event	Raw Score	Score	
PUSH-UP	30	48	DATE OF TEST 8 Aug	PUSH-UP	37	55	DATE OF TEST 22 Aug
SIT-UP	59	67		SIT-UP	53	76	
2-MILE RUN	18:39	14	PT RUN GROUP B	2-MILE RUN	14:10	77	PT RUN GROUP A

GO ☐ NG ☐ Counseling on back of form
GO ☒ NG ☐ Counseling on back of form

PART V ARMY VALUES Soldier displays/adopts Army Values to required level   **PART VI TENETS OF BCT** Begin to look, act, and think like a soldier

Exc	Good	Fair	Poor		
				LOYALTY	Bear true faith and allegiance to the US Constitution, the Army, your unit, and other soldiers.
				DUTY	Fulfill your obligations.
				RESPECT	Treat people as they should be treated.
				SELFLESS SERVICE	Put the welfare of the nation, the Army, and your subordinates before your own.
				HONOR	Live up to all the Army values.
				INTEGRITY	Do what is right, legally and morally.
				PERSONAL COURAGE	Face fear, danger, or adversity (Physical or Moral).

Exc	Good	Fair	Poor		
				Motivation	Expresses a commitment to succeed. Shows enthusiasm and puts forth maximum effort. A good influence on others.
				Appearance	Is neat and conscious of being in uniform.
				Adaptability	Is respectful towards superiors and tolerant of peers.
				Comprehension	Actively participates in training. Is attentive and asks questions. Shows understanding of training.
				Team Work	Seeks and gives help to peers. Accepts peer leaders.
				Self Discipline	Pushes self in training. Is trustworthy/responsible.
				Performance	Understands directions. Anticipates what is expected of self. Takes pride in individual task accomplishments.

GENERAL COMMENTS:

PART VII UCMJ/SICKCALLS/CODES Medical and Corrective actions   Excesses could result in NSO / Separation.

UCMJ: Summarized Company G. Field G. Reason:

Sickcall Date	Reason	Sickcall Date	Reason	Code	Dates on Code	#Days

DATE: 22 Aug 98   SOLDIER'S SIGNATURE: RATER'S SIGNATURE:

TRW Form 1113 (May 98) (Page 1 of 3)

Author's Progress Report received after passing his P.T. test.

sea of recruits flooded the streets.

There was no time to wait for Collins because I had to pass too, so I took off. Soaked in a bath of my salty sweat, I crossed the finish line in a time of fourteen minutes and twenty-seven seconds. I had passed comfortably, but Collins only had two more minutes to come in or he would fail. Powerless, I paced from side to side across the finish line, scanning my watch, waiting for my friend. Recruit after recruit passed on by as the time ticked, and with thirty seconds left, there was still no Collins. Out of nowhere came the ugliest shuffle of a run I had ever seen. The run belonged to Collins, whose ugly trot resembled a drunken penguin running from a walrus about to eat him. He was thirty feet away from the finish with ten seconds left. I began screaming at the top of my lungs, "You better run Collins! You only have eight seconds left!"

He kicked it into a moderately faster than slow gear, waddling ever so faster closer to the finish line. I jumped up and down, screaming as he got ever closer, and then he collapsed across the line and finished. I placed his arm around my shoulder and helped him to his feet. We walked over to the sideline to Drill Sergeant Spivey for his score. I found a spot over to the side, so that he would have his privacy. I peeked over in his direction as he got the news. He beamed with pride as he had run the fastest that he'd ever run in his life, but as Drill Sergeant Spivey spoke more, his demeanor slowly morphed into a slump, and then he wiped tears away from his eyes.

Collins didn't make it. He wiped his eyes a couple more times and came back over. He didn't wait for me to ask but volunteered the information. "He said I missed it by ten seconds. But he also said it was my fastest time." I replied, "That's great, man. I mean not great, but good news. At least you improved." He grinned and said, "Yeah. I get a do-over tomorrow."

I didn't ask what would happen if he didn't pass, but we only had a week left, so I knew.

I smiled at him and said, "You'll do it, bro."

He flashed me a half-hearted smile and replied, "I know. I gotta run back to my platoon, but I'll see you later."

We exchanged a man hug and he walked off. I never saw Collins again, as he failed his PT test the next day and was recycled. He didn't say goodbye to anyone. He just left, too ashamed to look me in the eyes. The sad reality of Basic is that not everyone makes it.

29

Bivouac

THERE WAS JUST A WEEK LEFT, BUT THE finish line seemed miles away. It was time for the big three-day bivouac FTX (Field Training Exercise.) It was the epitome of fun and the biggest thing that we had left to conquer. The purpose of the exercise was to give us a real world experience of being a soldier. We were mentally prepared for what to expect in briefings by our drill sergeants letting us know such things as:

-You will be gassed.
-If you lose any of the sensitive equipment, you will die.
-Prepare to be shot at by the enemy.
-You will sleep when you're dead.

All good things to know so close to the finish line.

Day 1: I was lucky, I guess, on the first day I was selected to an elite duty of packing all the supplies and guarding the weapons. The one perk of such an elite duty was that I got to miss the 10K road march that my fellow soldiers embarked on in the morning. By the time I got to the site in the evening, I was just in time to set up my tent and sleep. My platoon did not have guard duty so all around, it was the best day I had experienced thus far. *The FTX was a piece of cake, so what was the big deal*, I thought.

Day 2: In my life, nothing comes easy, so one great day must be balanced out in the ledger with an equally crappy one. That is what this day was. The next morning began with a bang. We woke with the dew and first things first, we had to brush our teeth, eat breakfast and camouflage our faces in an hour. Then we moved on to activities like building hasty firing positions and
classes. Just when you think the Army will take it easy on you, that is when it spices it up and by lunch time, things got extra spicy.

"GAS! GAS! GAS!"

Everyone donned masks in record time. Unfortunately, I had Nam flashbacks of Spruil in the gas chamber and struggled to get my mask on. I ended sipping some of the gas before slipping it on. The burn is like flames marching down your nasal passage and into your lungs with metal studs. Following suit, I transitioned into my MOPP gear (mission oriented protective posture.)

Of course, First Sergeant Snur came strolling out to

greet us wearing no mask, embracing the gas like flowers to the nose. He shouted to the company, "Listen up, soldiers. You will be eating lunch in your gas pajamas, so you're welcome. When you hear the all clear, you can remove the MOPP gear but not before. Again, you're welcome. Oh yeah, that all clear will come four hours from now, and in this heat it should feel like a slow roast. One last time, you're welcome."

Like I said, the scales must be balanced. I was convinced this was the longest day and couldn't possibly get worse, but as soon as I say that, it always does.

Four hours later and twenty pounds lighter from my sweat diet, we ate dinner. That meal probably ranked in my top twenty meals of all time and I can't even remember what I ate. My bliss was short-lived, however, as we had to prepare for the night that would never end. After building our two-man firing positions, we took our fighting positions. It was pitch black and we were not allowed to use our flashlights due to light noise discipline. Therefore, it was dark as hell! In true Khalid's life fashion, a storm came with lightning, thunder and the works. The setting was straight out of either of these movies: *Platoon* or *Apocalypse Now*.

The kicker of this exercise was, if the drill sergeants got to your tent and pretend-killed you, you might as well be real dead, as tomorrow you would have to answer to First Sergeant Snur. As the rain dropped in buckets, I waited. We all waited without a sound or movement with the vast empty forest ahead of us. I was paired with another, Meadders, an easy-going fella from Florida who made possibly the worst partner, because he was as scared sh!#less as me. Even though we were only armed with magazines of blanks, our shots would count. The enemy was wearing MILES gear (multiple integrated laser engagement system), so we were essentially playing a large scale game of laser tag. With that said, what do you get when you give ammo to soldiers scared witless? Itchy trigger fingers.

Crackle! Snap! Bang, bang, bang!!

The forest lit up like the Fourth of July. Suddenly everything seemed to be moving as our minds played tricks on us. That's when the screams started. They echoed in intervals of ten minutes, just long enough to think you were safe and short enough to keep your finger on the trigger. On top of all the stress, we were into the early morning now and had to fight sleep deprivation. It was not even a full day, but this was the first time.

My partner and I decided in order to cover more area, I would take the rear sight and he would take the front. It was perfect. We would never get caught by the enemy. For at least an hour, this plan calmed our nerves. We were on easy street now, so much so that we even added a wrinkle to our plan—alternating winks of sleep. This always seemed like a great plan, but it was often a young soldier's demise. As the sun shone on my face, I opened my eyelids and saw that my partner was opening his, too!

Day 3: In a panic, we looked around for any evidence that we had been caught. Our campsite was intact, but we knew that the real test would be at formation when they told us how we performed. Standing in formation, Meadders and I shot nervous bug-eyed glances at each other. First Sergeant Snur stepped in front of the formation with his smug smile and uttered these words: "Congrats that you completed your mission and defended your perimeter. Unfortunately, we have some of you that God wasted his time on creating and, therefore, endangered the whole Company. If I call your name, you can meet me in my tent. Because you're in deep doo-doo."

Name by name, he rattled off soldiers, and Meadders and I just knew we were done. Soldier after soldier hung his head until Snur abruptly stopped listing names. Meadders and I were not among them. Our smiles beamed as bright as the sun in disbelief that lady luck had smiled on us.

The third day was filled with packing up, cleaning the site and squad movements. The marquee attraction of the day was the night fire and 15K road march home. This was the last march, and at the end would be two days of rest and graduation. Dark approached quickly and evidence of our existence at the bivouac site was non-existent. Platoon after platoon lined up in rows of eight, ready for the last March. My knees shook. Dressed in full battle gear, I was hopeful my flat feet would hold up, as I battled with chronic foot problems.

A couple miles into the road march, I felt like Moses heading toward the promised land. Tree after tree looked like botanical clones of each other. We finally saw a fixture ahead. It was the night range. We stopped momentarily, drenched with sweat and blisters as we waited for our briefing. The drills explained to the group that we would be participating in a series of exercises while LIVE FIRE would be shot over our head. Yes, I said, LIVE FIRE! *That always sounds like a good idea.* After our briefing concluded, they set us on our way and we went live.

Ahead of us was a land that we had to conquer. It was equipped with barb wire, pits and tire runs. The one tip our drill gave us was to keep our heads low. *Reassuring.*

Having no place of real reference, I definitely felt we were starring in *Return of the Jedi* and the blasters were tracing over our heads. Between the bouts of anxiety, I would take a sec to admire the night sky illuminated with M-16 fire. It was beautiful in a chaotic Van Gogh "Starry Night" kinda way. The funny thing about things you are afraid of is fear only occupies the attentive mind. By the time I stopped admiring the light show, the range was over and I forgot why I was so scared in the first place.

At the conclusion of the range firing, we set off again, but this time we knew that at the finish line, we would be rewarded with milk and honey. Now all we had to do was the small thing of rucking this 10K with sixty pounds of gear on our backs. This was the equivalent of giving a dwarf a piggy back ride. Six kilometers into the march, the pressure on my feet finally took its toll, and with every step, it felt like nails were being pushed into my arch. When I was a Boy Scout, this same thing happened to me. I quit and that decision always haunted me. I vowed that this time would be different. As the march went on, the pick-up truck was picking up soldiers who couldn't make it left and right. I felt that maybe there was no shame in giving up. I couldn't feel my feet anymore and it felt that I was plopping my body weight on jelly. I surveyed the troops one more time, ready to give up, but in the crowd of soldiers, I saw my bunkmates and knew that they wouldn't give up, so I just couldn't. At that precise moment of uncertainty for me, my drill sergeant started shouting a cadence which, chanted in the right tone, can act as a rallying cry, rivaling the power of any *Rocky* movie. I began murmuring to myself an idiom that my drill sergeant ingrained into our soul, "Pain is just weakness leaving the body."

That saying took me over the top and I found rejuvenated legs. Not more than ten minutes later did I see the finish line populated with soldiers from our battalion, waiting for us. We had made it!

Once we crossed the finish line, a ceremony commenced honoring us with the Phase 3 guidon. This was a time honored tradition and our rites of passage. We were soldiers! Through the pain of this journey, I learned that your mind will quit way before your body. For a young man that had never been tried in this manner, learning mental fortitude was a journey of the soul that encompassed all nine weeks, culminating with this celebration.

30

Proud To Be an American

"**A**ND I'M PROUD TO BE AN AMERICAN where at least I know I'm free…"

If everyone in the building wasn't singing this as it played over the loudspeakers, you could call me a liar. I have never seen a building more patriotic than ours was that morning. For sixty-three days, this song had been our tormentor, rallying cry, beacon of hope and now, life anthem. So on this morning, a building filled with the shades, backgrounds, political views and religious beliefs of people at a United Nations meeting, we were one with synergy as we sang along to Lee Greenwood.

This day was one of the saddest and most joyful days that I have ever experienced in my life. For people that have never gone to battle with someone this might be hard to understand, but you have done something that, in your mind, seemed impossible up till then and you did it with a group of strangers that you had to depend on, and you achieved it. As the day went on, it was time to reflect and inhale the magnitude of our accomplishments. Everyone had some pep in their step as we cleaned and prepared our Class A uniforms. A Class A uniform was our equivalent of military fancy clothes. We were cruising, cracking jokes and dancing. We were so laid back, we decided to perform imitations of First Sergeant Snur. There was Jones, a tall, lanky kid from North Carolina, and he had Snur down to a tee. He ran from room to room, popping in and saying, "Hey, you son of a bitch, drop and give me fifty."

It was good old First Sergeant Snur's catch phrase. It worked every time. That is, until he jumped into a room without surveying the field and guess who was there? First Sergeant Snur!

He appeared from behind a bunk like a dark wizard, clapping slowly, and said in his nasally, scruffy voice, "Bravo. Bravo."

Jones couldn't take the words back fast enough before First Sergeant Snur declared, "You know what you need, private? A tutorial in killing yourself. Drop into the front lean and rest, and push until my mind gets tired."

That's how Private Jones spent his last day, but for the rest of us, that added to how much fun we were having. Even Jones knew it was worth it on the day we were getting out.

I hung out with my roommates on the last day. As we finished up squaring our room away, making our bunks, washing down the wall lockers and buffing the floor, we spent the time ribbing each other one last time. Malachi

The author's Class A uniform.

was the first one to start the roasting: "Saleem, remember when you and your battle buddy, Upchuck, pretended to die during shakedown, and you two got in trouble?"

Everyone broke out into laughter. I was the last one to eke out a smile, but it was water under the bridge. I wasn't going to be the butt of everyone's joke, so I jumped in too. "How 'bout you, Malachi? Do you remember the time the sergeant major found you hiding in the bushes after PT, huh?"

That drew another round of laughs from the guys. Of course, Malachi had to counter, "I was not hiding, but working smarter, not harder."

Thompson, who was our residential joker, took his slice too. "I know all you remember when Saleem had that garbage idea to flirt with that girl at PT. Then the drill sergeants ate his ass alive. It looked like one of those newborn wildebeest slaughters on a National Geographic video."

I couldn't help but be the first one to erupt with laughter. We had been through the ringer together and had made it. This went on with all of us getting a chance to punch in on each other. The morning flew by and before we knew, it was time for our graduation. We strutted outside for the final time in our dress uniforms and formed our platoons, ready to impress our families. Drill Sergeant Mitchell's toddler son was out there and greeted us as acting first sergeant. Someone thought it would be cute to put him out there. Now the drill sergeants wanted to get playful. The little boy called us to attention with his pipsqueak of a voice. Okay, maybe it was a little cute.

Then he said, "Half right face."

I was thinking, *Are you serious?* Then he commanded, "Front lean and rest position, move!"

And they were serious. He smoked us like it was nobody's business. Granted, the kid was cute and it was the last smoking we would ever get at Basic .

All the families loved it. My family was not there, however. We lived all the way in the Virgin Islands and I had asked them not to come. As corny as it sounds, I didn't feel like a boy anymore that needed his parents there to tell him how proud they were of him. This was not a knock on people who had their families there. I would have loved to have my parents by my side, but it just would have been too tough financially and not a necessity. After the sideshow of a smoking was over, they called us to attention. This was it. The time had finally come. We were going to graduate.

The field was decorated with red, white and blue streamers, the colors of our country.

Proud families with glistening smiles and pushed-out chests filled the bleachers. We marched up one platoon after the other; my 4th Platoon covered the rear. I looked around through my peripheral vision and my heart began to flutter with how many people were crying in the bleachers. I never grew up in this environment, so my patriotism went as far as chanting U.S.A. for the Dream Teams that played in the Olympics. This was something different. I was about to become married to the United States of America.

We were called to halt by the command sergeant major, who presented us to the audience and distinguished guests. A wave of pride rushed over me, and I pursed my lips and clenched my face to make sure I wouldn't shed any tears. The ceremony was validation that this journey was the toughest thing I had ever endured, but learning that if the journey was easy, then everyone would do it. Standing there, we were all vulnerable and on the verge of muscle failure. We were commanded into the parade rest for literally a half hour. Our legs were jittering and cramping at the same time, but through it all, we kept a

brave face on. We all knew how important this was and
none of us wanted to be that kid who fell out because his
little weak knees couldn't take it. We also had a little
extra dose of pride. How many times are you put on
display to an audience, exemplifying a microcosm of our
society?

A young me beamed with joy when the event happened,
but now an older version of me shed tears as I wrote this
passage, reminiscing on the moment that his life changed
for the better. It was the moment the command sergeant
major pronounced us all soldiers of the United States of
America that my heart grew ten times larger and so did
my ego. I felt invincible! I strutted up and down, meeting
all my friends' parents. I was a man, but the more I saw
friends with their families, the more I missed mine. I guess
even a man needs his mommy and daddy around
sometimes. That's when Drill Sergeant Mitchell caught me
and said, "Saleem, congratulations. I know your parents
aren't here today, but this letter came into the company for
you. Perfect timing."

I bit my lip to hide how much of a giddy, big kid I was
at that moment. She handed me the letter and walked
off. I waited for her to get out of sight and then I tore into
it. It read:

Dear Khalid, this is Mom and Dad, but mostly Dad. We
want you to know how proud of you we are and that we al-
ways knew you could do it. Okay, maybe not always. Ha
ha, but mostly. You are our most pragmatic and sensitive of
all our children, but you are also the most independent.
You made this decision all on your own and you stuck with

it. Like the day you beat me in chess, and I told you that you will never lose to me again because you had conquered that hurdle. This will be the same for you because when life gets unbearable, you won't look for the easy way out again and definitely won't let it beat you again. You will lean on this experience and it will serve as strength. We love you so much and can't wait to see you in December.

A picture of Mom, Dad, Jaleel, Amir, Scot and Zayd was attached on the bottom. I let the tears drop from my puffy eyes and cheeks this time. In the parking lot outside of Delta Company 110, it was time to depart for our various advanced individual training or AIT sites. Buses lined the lot, going to Ft. Sill, Oklahoma; Ft. Benning, Georgia; Ft. Jackson, South Carolina; and Ft.

Sam Houston, San Antonio, which was my AIT, or better known as freedom. Before jumping onto our buses, we all said our goodbyes. I ran up to my drill sergeant, Bauer, and shook his hand. Not because we were buddies. I actually had no idea who the man was personally. I thanked him for building me up. He looked me in the eyes and said something I will never forget: "I know we might have come off as hard asses, but our job is not to be your friend but to make sure you all become soldiers that protect our country."

I don't possess blind patriotism in my core, but what those words taught me was that we all have a responsibility in this life to help the youth in our country find their way. Some do it through fire and some with a cuddle, but at the end of the day, if you mold them with positive core values, you have improved them as human beings and help them

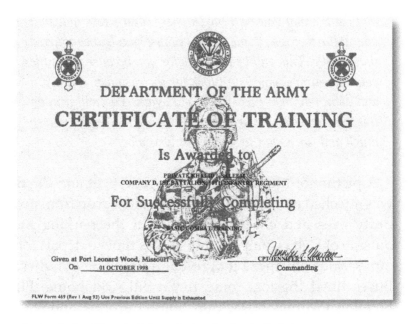

Author's Certificate of Completion for Basic Training.

survive and thrive in the world. I would love to say that when I hopped on my bus that day and left toward my AIT that I was a finished product as a man. But the truth is Basic Training is a building block and not the whole set. It would take many more years in the military for me to become that man, but that's a whole other story..

Acknowledgments

I WANT TO THANK ALLAH FOR BLESSING ME with a fortunate life. I want to thank my wonderful wife Kristel and two fabulous sons, Zavier and Azai, for being my giant pillars of support.

Thank you to my parents, Aminah and Abdullah, for love and guidance. Thank you to my parents in-law, Marjorie and Edwin Solomon, for belief. Thank you to my brothers, sisters, nephew, nieces, aunts, uncles and cousins: Abja, Scot, Amir, Zayd, Chris McGarity, James, Sonaya, Amenta, Natalie, Naisha, Naila, Joan, Cheleen, Kevy, Michael, Betty, Auntie, Kai, Cadence, Nadia, Al, Aaron, Michelle, Justin, Reggie, Kai, Charles, Marcus, Brian, Frank, Michelle, Chad, Mat, Josh, Brandon, Alicia, Jasmine, Kay, Viola, Shannon, Kirky, Chris, Dom Dom, Drew, Yannick, Miles, Troy, Lisa, Chelesse, Grandpa & Grandma Edwards, Dana, Liz, Devon, Daniel, Andrea, Sophie, Dr. Cohall, Desiree, Rui, Sammantha, Kayla, Clarissa, Kendra, Alex, Naomi, Jordan, Larry, Sul, Jason, Olympia, Gail, Henry, Lil Larry, Tanya, Marcia, Bobby,

Ida, Debi, Anna, Deborah, Debbie, Billy, Alley, Jerry, Ken, Seigo, Layla, Laurel, Tyrone, Yvette, Frank, Steve Biddick, and Debbie for the loving stories to write a million more books.

Thank you to my friends: Donald St. Anne, Sayi, Jen, Julita, Kim, Galacgac, Rachel, McCleary, Ramos, TJ, Vail, Sanders, Gina, Crews, Brigner, Johnson, Coleman, Joel, Egan, Seawright, Sanders, Churchill, Bell, Varner, Kameko, Austin, Fasthorse, Colon, Mullican, Reece, Terry, Hartley, Conklin, Acuna, Liza, Nicole, Schwarten, Mary Hampton, Elliot Johnson, McKenna, Pierce, Wiley, Vaughn, Erica, Chris Borodenko, LMAC, Jed, Jendayi, Jaime, Alscess Brown, Wallace, Razor, Kirby, Lawrence, Terrance, Kelson, Yamara, Margarita, Ibelize, Jenny, Joshua, Mr. & Ms. Gadd, Laurel, Aaron, Wilcox, Vicki, English, Ayanna, Sumi, Spears, Bullock, Jose, Mary, Oscar, Ms. Dye, Steals, Tatum, Foy, Jarrell, Daniels, Brown, Coyer, McClure, Mims, Staley, Foster, King, Meddlers, Blair, Robinson, Simmons, Jeannine, Williams, Craft, Campbell, Harrio, Watson, Wass, Delonica, Nayeli, Jordan, Anya, Payne, Dexter, Conly, Joe, Boyer, Riles, Mc'Fadden, Oaks, Newton, Frescoln, Anya, Kev, Aka, Reel, Sed, Neil, Liz, Amy, Tia, China, Karma, Seth, Angela, Anton, Dan, James, Carly, Heather, Paul, Aisha, Munesh, Sherzad, Jen, Steve, Virginia, Milz, Laura, Cathy, Mark, Noah Munoz, Sarah B, Suby, Tyler, Alex, McKena Aubrey, Megan Graff, Sam Maddox, Jennie Jarvis, Karishma, Sam, Jan Elf and Morgan. T hank you to my Basic Training battle buddies: Malachi, Henry Thompson, Katrice, Tran, Alma, Tia, and LeBlanc.

Thank you to my extended family: Messer, Good,

Felix, James, Campbell, O'reilly, Cohall, Edwards, Peterson, Phaire, Hepburn, Alvarado, and the Conde family.

Big thanks to: Complex 98! St.Croix Massive, V.I. Massive, National Guard, U.S. Army, and the whole military.

Lastly I'd like to say thank you to Christopher McGarity, Tanja Galetti, and Stacey Thompson for sparking this journey that has produced *Growing Up Green.*

About the Author

K HALID SALEEM IS A SCREENWRITER FROM the U.S. Virgin Islands who enlisted and served in the U.S. Army and served for ten years. During his time in the military he earned three Soldier of the Year awards from the various battalions in which he served. Khalid's passion for writing grew during his time in the military where the diverse society he was submerged in shaped his view on life, and provided him with rich stories to reflect on for years.

Khalid Saleem is a proud Screenwriting U alum, has earned a certificate from the UCLA Professional Program in Screenwriting, and has earned a Master of Fine Arts from Full Sail University. Khalid has a passion for comedy and writing children's books, and is the author of *The Circle*. His dream is to help other vets find a platform to share their rich experiences to help the youth of the world.

hellgatepress.com

CPSIA information can be obtained
at www.ICGtesting.com
Printed in the USA
LVHW040610171218
600723LV00018B/1444/P